Pacific Island Bastions of the United States

by HEROLD J. WIENS

Associate Professor of Geography
Yale University

A SEARCHLIGHT ORIGINAL
under the general editorship of

GEORGE W. HOFFMAN
University of Texas

G. ETZEL PEARCY
United States
Department of State

D. VAN NOSTRAND COMPANY, INC.

PRINCETON, NEW JERSEY

TORONTO

LONDON

NEW YORK

D. VAN NOSTRAND COMPANY, INC.
120 Alexander St., Princeton, New Jersey
(*Principal Office*)
24 West 40 Street, New York 18, New York

D. Van Nostrand Company, Ltd.
358, Kensington High Street, London, W.14, England

D. Van Nostrand Company (Canada), Ltd.
25 Hollinger Road, Toronto 16, Canada

Published simultaneously in Canada by
D. Van Nostrand Company (Canada), Ltd.

PRINTED IN THE UNITED STATES OF AMERICA

Preface

The United States frontage on two oceans inevitably has led to its greater military vulnerability on the one hand, and to its greater capacity for keeping potential enemies off its shores on the other. Naval power and, more recently, air power have been key elements in this two-sided picture. They have not and do not operate in a vacuum, of course. What is the nature of the space in which they have operated—its waters, skies, and scattered land areas? What conditions do naval and air power impose, what facilities do the installations built to serve them provide? Where do we find the conditions and facilities combined most favorably for the establishment of strategic bases to defend our shores from attack and to extend our striking power across the seas?

Who are the people on these islands? What do these islands contribute toward the support of population and what are their potentials? Is a crisis developing from growing population demands?

For which Pacific islands has the United States assumed responsibility as trustee? What is meant by the United Nations Strategic Trust Territories? What significant questions are posed by nuclear tests on them? In what way is the United States accountable to the United Nations for the Trust Territories? What roles do the islands play in the air communications net of the Pacific? Are the island bases obsolete in the nuclear and missile age? What sort of future development may be envisaged for the Pacific islands administered by the United States?

These are questions of vital interest to Americans concerned with the growth of the United States in international stature and with the security of their homeland. This book addresses itself to answering these questions and others related to them in order to help mature American citizens evaluate the role of the Pacific islands in this critical stage of United States history.

The approach to the strategic study of an area cannot be other than geographic. This book, therefore, stresses the physical environment and the cultural-political geography of the Pacific islands. It is hoped that the contents will prove valuable to teachers and students of political geography, international relations and military and naval science, as well as to government officials and the serious-minded public to whom the book is dedicated.

Hong Kong
January, 1962

HEROLD J. WIENS

Contents

List of Maps

I The Pacific Realm

In a truer sense than for any other nation, the North Pacific is a national ocean for the United States. An outer marginal line joining the limits of the islands of the Pacific under United States sovereignty and administration would enclose an area of some four-fifths of the North Pacific and almost half a million square miles of the South Pacific.

Within this enormous watery expanse, only the United Kingdom and New Zealand share control in a small part of the central Pacific, and Japan in the Bonin and Ryukyu chains. No other nation has administrative control over any island within this compass. In the South Pacific, by contrast, the numerous island groups form a crazy quilt of interspersed national sovereignties where France, the United Kingdom, the United States, New Zealand, Australia, the Kingdom of Tonga, soon-to-be-independent West Samoa and, in western New Guinea, the Netherlands, each exercise dominion. Beyond the periphery of these domains lie the Soviet-occupied Kuriles and the Asiatic islands of Japan, Taiwan, the Philippines and Indonesia.

SETTING THE BOUNDS

In the north the connecting points of the far-flung United States outer line begin with Tin City on Seward Peninsula in Alaska and pass through St. Lawrence Island in Bering Strait, both being about 60 miles from the Soviet Chukchee Peninsula. From here they run through Attu, the end island in the Aleutian chain, some 220 miles from the Soviet Komandorskie Islands. Almost a century has passed since the United States purchased the Alaskan territories from a Czarist Russia eager to dispose of them.

A two-thousand-mile expanse of landless water separates Attu from Marcus Island and from Muko Jima in the subtropical Bonin chain, the next cornerstones of the bounding line. From these islands the line runs west along about the 29th Parallel North to enclose the southern half of the Ryukyu Archipelago, with the key fortress and air base of Okinawa at the center of the chain. The Ryukyus bring the United States administration within 70 miles of our allies, the Republic of China on Taiwan, and less than 500 miles from Communist China's chief city of Shanghai.

This westward Asiatic salient was bought dearly with the blood of American G.I.'s in World War II and is retained under the Treaty of San Francisco, signed with Japan September 8, 1951. A further Japanese-American joint communiqué of June 21, 1957, announced the indefinite continuance of this control until tension subsides in Eastern Asia. However, the communiqué preserves Japan's inherent "residual sovereignty" in these islands. Included in the Asiatic salient are such small Japanese groups as the Bonin, Volcano, and Daito Islands and Parece Vela.

From the southern Ryukyus, the line runs southeast to the important naval and air base of Guam, enclosing all the islands of the Marianas to the north of it. This strategic advanced base lies 1229 miles from Okinawa, 1499 miles from Manila, and about 1700 miles from Tokyo. Ceded to the United States by Spain in 1899, the unincorporated territory of Guam in 1961 was still serving as the headquarters of the government of the Trust Territories of the Pacific Islands and of the United States Air Force's Strategic Air Command in the Pacific.

From here the outer boundary of United States administration runs southwest to approximately the 130th Meridian East, to contain the Western Carolines. These include such islands and groups as Ulithi Atoll in the northeast, Tobi Atoll in the southwest, and the volcanic islands of Palau and Yap in between. At Tobi the United States administration reaches within about 300 miles of Philippine Pulau-Pulau, 180 miles of Indonesian Morotai Island and 140 miles

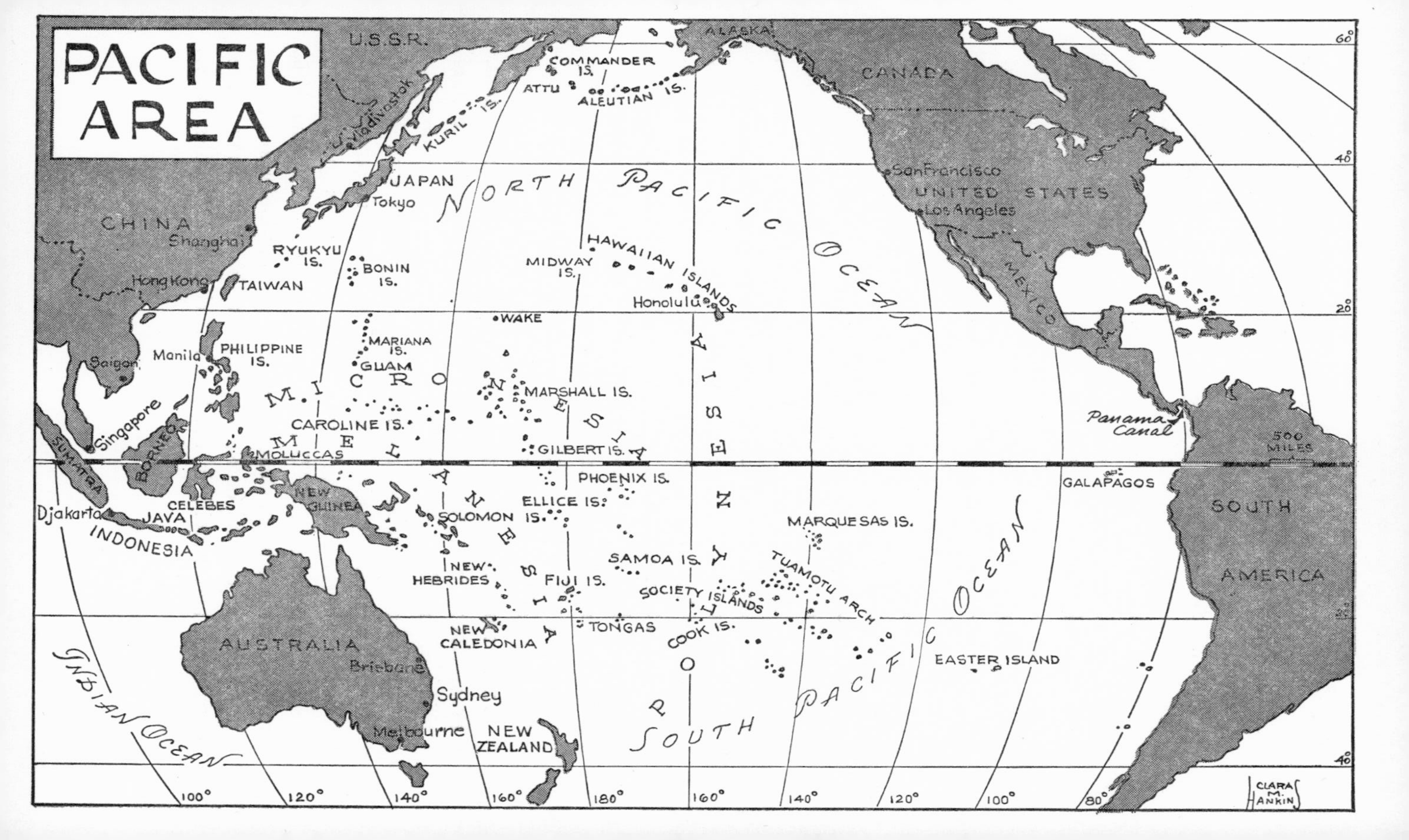
PACIFIC AREA
U.S.S.R.
CHINA
Shanghai
Hong Kong
Vladivostok
KURIL IS.
JAPAN
Tokyo
RYUKYU IS.
TAIWAN
BONIN IS.
PHILIPPINE IS.
Manila
Saigon
Singapore
SUMATRA
BORNEO
CELEBES
JAVA
Djakarta
INDONESIA
MOLUCCAS
NEW GUINEA
MARIANA IS.
GUAM
CAROLINE IS.
MICRONESIA
MELANESIA
POLYNESIA
WAKE
MARSHALL IS.
GILBERT IS.
COMMANDER IS.
ATTU
ALEUTIAN IS.
ALASKA
MIDWAY IS.
HAWAIIAN ISLANDS
Honolulu
NORTH PACIFIC OCEAN
CANADA
UNITED STATES
San Francisco
Los Angeles
MEXICO
Panama Canal
500 MILES
GALAPAGOS
SOUTH AMERICA
PHOENIX IS.
ELLICE IS.
SOLOMON IS.
NEW HEBRIDES
FIJI IS.
SAMOA IS.
TONGAS
SOCIETY ISLANDS
COOK IS.
MARQUESAS IS.
TUAMOTU ARCH
EASTER ISLAND
SOUTH PACIFIC OCEAN
NEW CALEDONIA
AUSTRALIA
Brisbane
Sydney
Melbourne
NEW ZEALAND
INDIAN OCEAN
60°
40°
20°
40°
100°
120°
140°
160°
180°
160°
140°
120°
100°
80°
CLARA M. HANKINS

of the Dutch-held Asia Islands north of the bird's head of New Guinea.

For two thousand miles the latitudinally oriented Caroline archipelago stretches from the coral atoll of Pulo Anna in the west to volcanic Kusaie Island in the east. All of these islands form part of the strategic Trust Territory of the Pacific Islands. The southernmost island, 65 miles north of the Equator, is that delightfully named Polynesian atoll of Kapingamarangi.

To the east the Carolines almost join the two parallel northwest-to-southeast-running chains of the Marshalls, also part of the Trust Territory. In the middle of the Marshalls sprawls Kwajalein, the largest atoll in the world, providentially providing a strategic air base and naval anchorages.

At Mili in the southeasternmost of these atolls, the bounding line turns southeastward to cross the Equator and to reach 1800 miles to eastern Samoa. This extremity lies a thousand miles south of the Equator. From it the final leg of the enclosing line connects the former naval base at Tutuila Island with the United States naval base at San Diego, California, across 4200 miles of watery wastes.

North of Samoa are such jointly U.S.-U.K.-administered islands as Canton and Enderbury and the disputed islands of the Line and Phoenix groups. In the latter the atoll of Canton forms an important commercial refueling air stop for flights between Hawaii and the "down under" lands of Australia and New Zealand.

In the center of these great ocean spaces sit the Hawaiian Islands. From Honolulu a web of sea and air lanes radiates to the chief points of the North Pacific rim and the chief island centers. The lengths of the main sea strands of this web provide some idea of Hawaii's strategic situation at its center, rivaled by no other island group in the Pacific. San Francisco lies 2091 miles to the east. Seward in Alaska lies 2373 miles to the northeast, Panama 4685 miles to the southeast. Petropavlovsk, the Soviet Union's strategic naval base at the end of Kamchatka, lies 2762 miles away to the northwest, and Tutuila in the South Pacific is 2276 miles away.

Westward it is about 2500 miles to Kwajalein, 3318 miles to Guam, 3397 miles to Tokyo, about 4500 miles to Okinawa, and 4817 miles to Manila.

This scattered island empire constitutes the administrative responsibility of the United States in the Pacific and the sphere of our discussion. Among the islands there stand some major bastions protecting the security of the United States and of the free world. Other islands are links in the communications chains that facilitate world and interisland commerce. Still others demand the educational, financial, and economic subsidy of the United States for progress in the modern world, its political tutelage for development of democratic self-government, and its protection for peaceful and prosperous existence.

THE PACIFIC: A BUFFER, A SEAWAY, AN AIR ROUTE

Although the natural geography of the Pacific remains much the same as it has been for thousands of years, its communications character has passed through five stages during the last thousand years. Two of these have been experienced during the last hundred years.

The first period was the prehistoric period before the use of seaworthy craft, when the ocean expanses proved an absolute barrier, and only chance or storm brought a forlorn and rare castaway from one island to another. The second period began with early Malayan, Micronesian, Melanesian and, particularly, Polynesian navigation, when the tropical and subtropical Pacific islands were settled. The Pacific was first spanned then by Polynesians who somehow made their way to and from South America at an unknown date after A.D. 1000, when they brought the sweet potato from South America to Polynesia.

The third period inaugurated the large European-type and first truly trans-Pacific sailing ship. This era began with the voyage of Magellan in 1521 and lasted through the first half of the nineteenth century. During this period the Pacific was regarded more as something to be crossed than as an area in which to settle. Only a few small attempts were made to settle Europeans in some islands of the West Pacific, particularly Guam, the Philippines, and parts of Indonesia.

The fourth period began with the steamship, which freed the sea lanes from complete dependence upon the Pacific wind systems and brought significant international rivalry among European powers, the United States, and Japan for control of the Pacific islands.

Perhaps the fifth period should date from the first trans-Pacific flight of an airplane under United States Army pilots, who in 1927 flew from Oakland, California, to Honolulu, Hawaii. It certainly was under way by the time of the epic and tragic flight of Amelia Earhart, a pioneer in Pacific flight whose mysterious disappearance in the vicinity of the Truk Islands a few years before Japan's attack on Pearl Harbor foreshadowed the mighty role that aircraft were to have in the Pacific future, both miltary and commercial.

During the first of the five stages, dating from the dawn of man in the Pacific fringe, the role of the Pacific was that of an obstacle and buffer to intercontinental and interisland contacts. Each succeeding stage has diminished the ocean's role as an obstacle and enhanced its functions as a freeway of communications. However, the Pacific as a buffer has remained highly significant, and it continues to interpose difficulties to contacts. For many small islands of Micronesia and Polynesia the development of larger, modern steamships and aircraft paradoxically has resulted in deteriorated interisland communications. Inability of native boats to compete with modern ships in the carriage traffic has led to abandonment of onetime sea-navigation routes and of seagoing boat construction. At the same time, the economics of modern shipping inhibits frequent calls of ships at scattered small islands with little freight to offer and few demands for service.

II *Pursuers of the Sunrise: Eastward Migrants from Asia*

Just when the first prehistoric "Asiatic Balboa" overlooked the Pacific from its western shores to wonder what lay beyond the horizon can never be ascertained. It is known, however, that early man had reached the Indonesian and Philippine Islands, probably by land bridges, a quarter of a million years ago. In the Philippines, the fossil remains of the contemporaries of the Java man accompany the bones of the *Stegodon* elephants and rhinoceros where all of these became extinct before the ice ages. We are more concerned with the culture bearers who followed in wave after wave of migrants seeking lands of the dawn over the Pacific. The primary routes of migration in the west Pacific have been eastward and northward, with minor movements from the northwest Pacific. In the central Pacific, the movement was eastward, then northward and southward, with minor waves moving as a kind of backwash westward into Melanesia.

The links in the chains of islands from Indonesia to southern Japan are relatively close together, facilitating the movements of people into them from southeastern Asia and south China from prehistoric times. The seasonal north-south monsoon winds and the China Seas currents driven by these winds effectively aided these migratory movements. No doubt, also, on frequent occasions storms drove unwilling canoe or boat occupants from mainland coastal areas to new islands in these chains, or from one island to another. The size and the high elevations of many of the islands in these chains make them visible to navigators from great distances. There are many peaks over 8000 and 9000 feet high in the Philippines, and in Taiwan (Formosa) several dozen peaks rise to over 10,000 feet. Palawan Island and the Sulu archipelago form convenient bridges from Borneo to Luzon and Mindanao in the Phillippines. Across the waters from Luzon to Taiwan stretch the Bataan and Lanyu Islands. Between no two adjoining islands is the water gap greater than about 50 miles. Only between Okinawa and Miyako in the southern Ryukyus does the water gap exceed this distance in the entire stretch of islands from Borneo to Kyushu, Japan, and here it widens to about 180 miles.

WAVES OF MIGRATION

The oldest of the migratory waves sweeping through the Indonesian realm came some 50,000 years ago. This wave then moved northward through the Philippines, possibly as far north as Taiwan, comprising primitive negritos whose relatives are found in such far-scattered regions as India and South Africa. A second wave of a larger-statured negroid group moved eastward out of Southeast Asia into and past New Guinea to as far east as New Caledonia. Representatives of this group, however, did not move northward into the Philippines. This culturally more advanced group of fuzzy-haired, coarse-featured negroids was followed by a third negroid group, sometimes called the higher Melanesians because of their still more advanced culture. The latter stood in stature between the negrito and the second group of negroids. The third group became the inhabitants of the island coasts and were canoe builders and fishers, coconut and taro growers, and keepers of pigs and chickens —and also were cannibals.

Into the Philippines the migratory waves of negritos and other primitive proto-Malay Australoids began 25,000 to 30,000 years ago, with the last waves some 12,000 to 15,000 years ago. Their descendants form about one-half of one per cent of the contemporary Philippine population, mostly inhabiting areas east of the mountain axis from Mindanao to Luzon. Perhaps three or four thousand years B.C. saw immigrants of a new type, classified as early Indonesian or

Malay of the New Stone Age. They were builders of thatched wooden-frame houses set over shallow pits, and they used stone axes and adzes and grew millets and yams. Their impact upon the present population is said to be exhibited in the 12 per cent of the Philippine population who are their descendants.

Beginning about 1500 B.C. a new inpouring of immigrant peoples surged into the Philippines from present-day Vietnam and the South China coast. These introduced upland rice and new varieties of yams. The new immigrants were planters of taro and were dry-field cultivators. Other cultural traits brought by them were the use of jadite or nephrite tools, beaten bark cloth intricately decorated with block-printed designs, and pyramidal roofs set on posts above-ground. While these culture bearers trickled into the Philippines for a thousand years, it would appear that wet-rice cultivation was brought eastward as early as 800 B.C. across the South China Sea into the Indonesian realm by Early Bronze Age Indonesians. They built elaborate terraces and introduced mainland Asiatic methods of copper mining and smelting and bronze forging. Representatives of at least the first of these two groups advanced northward into Taiwan.

The last of the prehistoric migratory waves of Asians moved northward through present-day Indonesia in fleets of dugout canoes. From the west coast of Borneo they penetrated into Palawan and Mindoro and thence into Luzon. Their descendants are the most numerous of the Philippine ethnic groups today, the modern Malay Filipino representing some 37 per cent of today's population of about 24 million people. They brought with them the horse and carabao as work animals, and they knew the arts of iron smelting and working, of weaving on looms, and of green and blue glass bead manufacture for bracelets. They made and decorated pottery. Some of their arts were carried northward by person or trade into Taiwan, the Ryukyus, southern Japan, Korea, and even Manchuria. They may properly be considered to have an advanced civilization.

Some 20 per cent of the Philippine population apparently are descendants of immigrants of the last two thousand years, including elements of Hindu, Arab and Persian origins, as well as large numbers of Chinese and some European and American settlers. The first recorded ship to sail to China was from Mindoro in A.D. 982. A trade and tribute embassy to China sailed from Luzon in 1372, and thereafter contacts with the Chinese became frequent. Today possibly a million Philippine inhabitants have Chinese or part-Chinese blood.

SETTLERS OF TAIWAN

In Taiwan the northward movement of peoples via Indonesia and the Philippines did not produce as great a mixture as in the Philippines. Until the Chinese migrations into the island following the Manchu conquest of China in 1644, most of the islanders were relatively pure early Indonesians without the numerous cultural overlays that have occurred in the Philippines and in Indonesia. Thus, in Taiwan there are preserved among some of the un-Sinicized tribes traits of the older cultural stratum of Indonesia. Their strongholds remain in the interior mountains and east coast regions of Taiwan. Of the 200,000 Taiwan people of Indonesian origin, about a quarter have been absorbed into Chinese life and customs. Among the remaining 155,000 people, divided into nine ethnic groups in 1950, the Ami, with 50,000 members, the Atayal, with 36,000, and the Paiwan, with 32,000, were the leading tribal groups. The other groups number from as many as 18,000 (the Bunun) to as few as 1400 (the Yami).

Although Taiwan was known to the Chinese before the Christian era, little attention was paid to it until 605 or 606 A.D., when occasional contacts began to be made. Settlements by Chinese were made in the fourteenth century on Taiwan, but they were abandoned in the middle of the seventeenth century. The Indonesian tribesmen of the island continued to dominate the land even after Spanish and Portuguese contacts, and it was the Portuguese who gave it the name "beautiful"—*formosa*. Dutch traders who built a fort on the southwest coast in 1624 were driven out by a Chinese adventurer, Koxinga, in 1661.

Koxinga turned from piracy to patriotism in support of the native Ming dynasty of China in futile efforts to defend its empire against the invading Manchu. For twenty years after the Manchu gained the throne of China, he continued to ravage the South China coast from his base on Taiwan. After his death Taiwan reverted peaceably to the mainland government, and regular colonization of the island by Chinese began to take place. Chinese soon outnumbered the indigenous Indonesian tribespeople, and by 1935 their numbers had reached about five million.

Taiwan's occupation by Japan as a prize of the 1894 Sino-Japanese War lasted fifty years. The half-million Japanese residents controlled the administration and economy, but the growing Chinese population by the end of World War II had reached six million. The Japanese residents were removed in 1945, but a new wave of mainlanders fleeing from Communist conquest of China swelled Taiwan's population by 1½ million during 1945-46. Today's (1961) population of over 10 million in Taiwan is 98 per cent Chinese, largely derived from the Fukien and Kwangtung coastal provinces.

RYUKYUAN ORIGINS

Northward from Taiwan the Ryukyu Islands form the natural migration route for people from south China and Taiwan. Little is known of the early peoples of this archipelago, but there are evidences that in the Ryukyus the northward movement met the southward movement of north Asian people. There are affinities that link the Ryukyuans with both north and south. However, it is believed that the earliest inhabitants were the Neolithic Caucasoid Ainu whose penetration of the archipelago may have resulted from their flight from the Yamato occupation of Kyushu in southern Japan. Thus, whereas the upper classes of people in these islands closely resemble the Japanese probably because of intermarriage, the lower social groups are shorter than the Japanese, have higher foreheads, less deeply set eyes, less flattened faces, and greater hairiness, with thicker arched eyebrows. Hairiness, especially, is associated with Ainu characteristics as absence of body hair is associated with the Mongoloid traits.

The earliest written accounts of contacts with China date to 608 A.D. Japanese ships reached the northern Ryukyus in 689 and Okinawa in 743. By the twelfth century a native dynasty with mythical Japanese connections had been founded. Closer relations with China came during the fourteenth century and with Japan during the fifteenth century, so that the Sino-Japanese character of the Ryukyuan civilization and its over 800,000 people (1956) has become firmly established.

This, then, is a brief account of the migratory movements that have peopled the southern volcanic arcs of islands enclosing the China Seas. These are the peoples who are allies of the United States in the struggle against Communist conquest. Their ties with Asiatic cultures are strong and they represent the main stream of the eastward surge of peoples toward the maritime lands of the sunrise from the Asiatic continent.

MIGRANTS TO MICRONESIA

Having traced the human migratory waves eastward to the limits of the China Seas, let us inquire how they progressed farther into the Micronesian and Polynesian chains beyond, until they finally penetrated what became the fiftieth State of the United States. When did men first enter these realms and what manner of men were they? The dating of the presence of man is done by a great variety of anthropological, archeological, and scientific devices to which the tool of radio-carbon dating has added a most useful method. From a site study on Saipan it has been concluded that man had established residence in this part of the Marianas by 1500 B.C. Probably the Western Carolines were settled by this time also, since it seems more reasonable to suppose that man arrived at Saipan via the Yap and Palau chains in the south than via the Bonins in the north. However, carbon dates need to be determined for the Palaus and Yap and for such areas as Truk and Ponape before definite confirmation can be made of such a great age for man in these Carolinian islands.

Were these early "Micronesians" related to the proto-Malay Australoids or negritos who entered the Philippines between 30,000 and 12,000 B.C.? Whether they came then or later, negrito elements related to the negrito found on Bataan and elsewhere in Luzon are present in Yap Island and the Palau Archipelago. Or were the earliest immigrants similar to those that entered into the Philippines about 1500 B.C.? While these people grew yams and cultivated taro just as the present-day Micronesians do, they also introduced upland rice into the Philippines, and this trait is not found among the early Carolinians and Marianas people, so far as is known. It is not likely that so important and easily transported a food and seed-stock would have been left behind in the migration eastward from the Philippines or Indonesia, had the migrants possessed this culture.

The cultural characteristics of the earliest peoples in Micronesia are hardly known. They must have had sailing canoes of some type in order to get where they settled. They may have carried the coconut, taro and yam with them to plant in the new islands, but this conjecture must remain based upon reasonable assumptions. The physical and racial characteristics show complex intermixtures and differences, even within most of the individual islands. In addition to the obvious Mongoloid traits (especially common at Kusaie in the extreme east end of the Carolines), negrito traits (most noticeable on Yap and the Palau Islands), as well as some Polynesian characteristics, a so-called "generalized" Micronesian strain appears to apply throughout the Marshalls and Carolines and especially around Ponape.

Recognition of the different physical types gives but faint clues to their origins and tells little about the time or chronology of their entry into the Micronesian theater. We are safe in stating that racial and cultural traits link western Micronesia with the Philippines and Indonesia, southern Micronesia with Melanesia and New Guinea and eastern Micronesia with Polynesia.

POLYNESIAN VOYAGERS

For the latest early ethnic group of migrants to pursue the sunrise over the Pacific we have more information. Their recency has permitted the preservation with a high degree of reliability of the oral traditions of their travels, at least within the confines of their present realm, Polynesia. Many other lines of anthropological inquiry, however, provide convincing evidence that they, too, came from or traveled through Southeast Asia. Blood types, linguistic kinship, cultural relationships, traditions and myths all place their origin in the west. The raft expeditions of Thor Heyerdahl on the *Kon-Tiki* in 1947 and the similar expeditions of Eric de Bisschop in both directions on the *Tahiti Nui* I and II in 1957 and 1958 have demonstrated the possibilities of ocean drift in human contacts between South America and the Polynesian lands, but they have not upset the theory of Polynesian migration from southeast Asia, which appears to be far better grounded.

Two important queries concerning the Polynesians, then, concern the time of their voyaging and the routes they traveled. It is obvious that if the Polynesians came from the west, they must have used the Micronesian or Melanesian islands as stepping stones in their progress. From negative evidences, various anthropologists have ruled out the Melanesian route. In their advance into the eastern island groups, the Polynesians would have stayed long enough on the different islands en route to leave cultural influences behind and to pick up significant cultural traits which they took with them. On both of these scores, it appears clear that the Polynesians moved eastward through the Caroline Islands. Their probable paths of migration into the so-called Polynesian triangle bounded by lines connecting the three corners at Hawaii, New Zealand, and Easter Island are shown on charts in most studies of the subject.

It is believed that after reaching the Marshalls, one line of Polynesian migration may have gone directly northeast to Hawaii, the main stream following the Gilberts to the Society Islands and another stream turning south through the Ellices to Samoa. From both of these centers, further dispersions occurred, the major dispersion being from the Society group. Estimations from genealogical records orally handed down and going back to the times of the first settlement of these areas and from the amount of change in dialects since settlement make it appear that the major dispersals took place in eastern Polynesia between 900 and 1250 A.D. It also has been estimated that prior to the great dispersal there may have been a period of some 500 years of habitation in eastern Polynesia, during which time characteristic features held in common in eastern Polynesia developed. Before the Polynesians got to Tahiti and the rest of the Societies, their protracted habitation in western Polynesia may have been even longer. These speculative assumptions would have the first wave of Polynesians moving through the Carolines and Marshalls as early as the turn of the Christian era and their movement out of Indonesia in B.C. times.

The name Havaii, recalling earlier homelands in the west, has been applied to a number of settlement centers of Polynesia, especially Raiätea in the Societies west of Tahiti. Others include Hawaiki in New Zealand, Avaiki in the Cook Islands, Savai'i in Western Samoa, and, of course, our fiftieth State of Hawaii. Raiätea was the earliest center of priestly learning, apparently, and from here proceeded the voyages of discovery and dispersion that reached northward into Hawaii, eastward and southeastward through the Tuamotus to Easter Island, southward to the Australs and Rapa, and southeastward to the Cooks and New Zealand. It is believed to be fairly certain that most of these island groups had been discovered and settled by 1000 A.D.; the extensive settlement of New Zealand is believed to have occurred about 1350. Mangareva apparently was first discovered from the Marquesas. The contact with Peru that brought back the *kumar* or *kumara* (sweet potato) may also have come from the Marquesas.

One anomaly in Micronesia and the northeastern and northern fringes of Melanesia needs explanation. This is the presence of several low islands or coral atolls inhibited by people with Polynesian cultures. In Micronesia they are the atolls of Nukuoro and Kapingamarangi. In the Melanesian fringe the atolls of Ontong Java, Sikiana, and Nuguria northeast of the Solomons and Bellona and Rennell south of Guadalcanal are strongly Polynesian both linguistically and culturally. Ticopia in the southern Santa Cruz Islands and several atolls in the Lau group of the eastern Fijis also are strongly Polynesian in character. The racial type in Ontong Java, however, is Micronesian. The position of all these atolls on the northeast fringes of Melanesia, and other anthropological features as well, point to a westward wave of Polynesian migration from Samoa and Tonga. Some of this movement was purposeful, but no doubt the original settlement of other islands here was accidental, by occupants of canoes driven westward by storm winds and ocean currents.

Whatever the chronology of the various migratory waves of Micronesians and Polynesians in the western, central and south Pacific, there is no doubt that almost every bit of land in the tropical Pacific had been discovered and the desirable bits settled by these intrepid canoe voyagers sailing toward the lands of the sunrise long before European explorers discovered them for their sponsoring countries. Their single voyages were not as long as those of the Europeans, who for the most part came in the opposite direction across the Pacific with favorable currents and winds. Their records, however, especially considering their small craft on the open ocean, are even more impressive.

LINGUISTIC KINSHIPS

Micronesia and Polynesia share linguistic kinship with the Indonesian realm that joins them all in one linguistic family: the Malay-Polynesian language. Within this family, differences comparable to those among the Romance languages create difficulties of intercommunications. Among the Polynesian groups the diversity is not as great as among the Micronesian languages, where sharp differences occur. The western Micronesian Yapese, Palauan and Chamorro appear to be closer to certain Philippine languages than to tongues spoken farther east in Micronesia. East of Yap and the Palaus, the islanders speak languages that have been described as

Nuclear Micronesian, centering on Truk and Ponape. The most divergent members of this group are considered to be the languages of Kusaie, the Marshalls and the Gilberts. The Polynesian exceptions at Nukuoro and Kapingamarangi are notable.

ISLAND POLITICAL ORGANIZATION

Political organizations among the numerous small islands of Micronesia and Polynesia were limited to relatively small spheres of influence. The tightest organizations and the strongest social differentiation between rulers and ruled occurred in the larger volcanic island groups such as Hawaii, the Societies and the Tongas, although the New Zealand society was more like the democratic forms of the smaller islands. Political ties among the smaller scattered islands often were very loose, although certain paramount chiefs in the Marshalls received allegiance and tribute from a large number of islands. Some of the isolated atolls were little worlds in themselves, having no outside connections and often only rare outside contacts in early periods. No central kings ruled over large regions of the Pacific or tried to unite all or even large parts of Polynesia or Micronesia, and a national sense has never been developed on a widespread scale.

In most cases each island was its own concern, and even in such a closely related group as the Marshalls, people on one atoll until recent years cared little about what happened to people on another, unless they had relatives living there. Under such circumstances it is not hard to see why the islands and their inhabitants fell easy prey to successive conquerers, adventurers and slavers. It is equally easy to understand why present-day efforts to bring groups of islands into a uniform political administration meet so many difficulties. Traditional political-cultural structures, the great distances separating the multitude of island units, and the time and cost of transportation militate against such attempts.

III *Disciples of Magellan: Europeans in the Pacific*

WHILE the pioneer settlers of Micronesia and Polynesia were spreading out over the large island realms of the Pacific, neither Asian nor European countries were aware of their existence or of the existence of the hundreds of scattered islands on which they made their homes. In this sense, then, the European explorers in the Pacific were the first discoverers of these islands and their peoples for the "civilized world." By the fourteenth century, many of the Polynesian leaders at such centers as Tahiti and Samoa had a great amount of knowledge of the geographic distribution of islands in their realms. Within a more restricted zone around their main centers, some Micronesian chiefs and navigators also knew the general location of large numbers of islands and island groups about their homelands. Interisland communication for trade, tribute, and warfare was not uncommon. The first European explorer, however, had to start from scratch, although many of them managed to gather information about islands not yet visited by questioning the people they discovered. European motives in such explorations also were quite different from those of the early Micronesian and Polynesian explorers, and they proceeded in a much more organized and purposeful manner. Europeans came to the Pacific for reasons relating to trade, religious proselyting, economic exploitation, and empire building, rather than to find new homesteads.

In examining the course of European activities in the Pacific, one can perceive certain chronological groupings that divide the time span before the twentieth century into four periods. With broad historical license, these may be conveniently classified by successive centuries beginning with 1500. The first, from 1500 to 1600, was the period of Spanish-Portuguese exploration. The second, 1600 to 1700, was the period of Dutch trading settlements. The third, 1700 to 1800, covers the period of French and English exploration. The nineteenth century may be termed the period of close contact between Pacific islanders and Europeans and Americans, and the beginning of empires in the Pacific.

SPANISH-PORTUGUESE EXPLORATION

The Portuguese did not seriously challenge the Spanish in the Pacific, because in the arbiration of rival claims in the Catholic fold the decision of the Pope and the Treaty of Tordesillas of 1494 awarded the sphere of interest in the Pacific to the Spaniards. In 1513, when Balboa reached a point overlooking the Pacific, he claimed it for Spain. Actually the Portuguese saw the ocean from the west before Balboa did, and Magellan himself took part in expeditions around Africa and past India to the Moluccas in 1511. Nevertheless, when Magellan decided to reach these Spice Islands by navigating around South America and across the Pacific from the east in 1519, he was doing this in the service of Spain. Unfortunately for him, Magellan mostly discovered the gaps between islands, seeing only two poorly identified islands in eastern Polynesia before hitting upon Guam on March 6, 1521. But he went on to find the Philippines, which he named after Philip II. Although he lost his life here, the lasting effect of his discovery is testified to by the predominantly Catholic character of their population today.

Further interest in Pacific exploration from the east did not occur until Cortez and Pizarro had established themselves in Mexico and Peru respectively. It was forty-six years after Magellan reached Guam that another Spanish expedition sailed across the Pacific, this time from Callao, Peru, under Alvaro Mendaña. This venture probably was the outcome of the discovery by Andres de Urdaneta that a ship sailing northward from Manila until it reached the westerlies could successfully make the eastward crossing of the Pacific to reach the New World. Mendaña also missed seeing any of the islands of Polynesia except one of the Ellice Islands; he reached his first land at Santa Isabella in the Solomons after seeing Ontong Java in passing. Since the primitive people here yielded no spices, gold, silver, "nor of any other source of profit," his Spanish superiors were not excited by his discovery and paid little attention to this area.

A second voyage by Mendaña with his pilot Pedro Fernandez de Quiros discovered some of the Marquesas (named after the Marquesas de Mendoza). He sailed further west to discover the Santa Cruz Islands, which he thought were the Solomons discovered twenty-eight years before. On his return via the westerlies he found Wake Atoll.

His pilot Quiros in 1606 made a colonizing voyage to Melanesia, discovering some small islands in eastern Polynesia en route, but his colony on Espiritu Santo broke up because of mutiny, disease, and trouble with the Melanesians. While Quiros gave up and returned to Mexico, his pilot Torres sailed westward to discover the present Torres Strait between New Guinea and Australia before turning north to reach Manila via the Ceram and Celebes seas. Although the Spanish by this time had lost interest in exploration and were content to develop the Philippines and their New World empires, they did not wish any rival nation to benefit from their knowledge and buried their discoveries in official archives.

DUTCH VENTURES IN THE PACIFIC

Dutch navigators in the service of Spain, when Holland was part of the Spanish empire, became acquainted with the regions of Spanish exploration. On the basis of their experiences with the Spanish, they published charts of the East Indies and of the Far East. Subsequently, independent Dutch merchants, jealous of the East India Company's monopoly of the Indies trade, tried to discover other trading areas by sailing west around South America. The voyage of Jakob Le Maire and his pilot William Schouten across the South Pacific brought about the discovery of the Admiralty and

Schouten Islands. En route in 1616, they passed through the Tuamotu group and discovered Hoorn or Futuna Islands between the Samoas and the Fijis. However, these small islands and primitive cultures did not provide the commercial incentives necessary to interest the Dutch merchants. It was more than a century later that a Dutch concern, the West India Company, sent another expedition via Cape Horn to explore the Pacific east of the East India Company's territory. In 1721-22 Jacob Roggeveen followed somewhat the same general route of Schouten and Le Maire, discovering Easter, which he named, several islands in the Tuamotus and Societies, and Tutuila and Opolu in Samoa.

More significant exploration was done by Janszoon Tasman, who sailed from the west under the sponsorship of the Dutch East Indies Company in 1642. He not only discovered Tasmania and New Zealand, whose names reflect their Dutch origin, but in his northward voyage from New Zealand, he found the Tongas and Fijis. Aside from his explorations along the north shores of New Guinea on this trip, Tasman made another voyage in 1644 that traced the north and west coasts of Australia. In contrast to the secretive Spanish, the Dutch were free in publicizing their discoveries.

FRENCH AND BRITISH VOYAGES

For half a century after Tasman, little significant exploration occurred in the central and west Pacific. The end of the seventeenth century marked the entry of Great Britain into the Pacific islands world. Between 1695 and 1726 many scores of British and French voyages were made into the Pacific by sea rovers and freebooters, largely to prey upon Spanish galleons. However, they added little in the way of discovery of unknown lands. One of these, a sometime buccaneer and sometime officer of the Royal Navy and merchant navigator, was William Dampier. More enterprising than some, he discovered New Britain and the strait that bears his name. But his writings stirred greater interest than his discoveries. Speculations concerning a vast unknown southern continent termed Terra Australis Incognita stimulated governments to exploration, and George III of Great Britain became personally interested in it. The eighteenth-century exploration by the British became a "sustained attempt" to secure British ascendancy in the South Sea, according to one British author.[1] This was also a period of scientific interest in the Pacific. It was during Lord Anson's circumnavigation of the globe in 1740-1744 that knowledge of a remedy for scurvy was discovered by Dr. James Lind through his study of this scourge of maritime travel. With this knowledge, Captain Cook was able to prevent the heavy losses that previously had plagued mariners on long sea trips. No doubt this advance contributed to his success as the leading explorer of the Pacific.

The peace settlement in Europe that followed the Treaty of Paris in 1763 opened the way for British and French scientific explorations of the Pacific. Commodore John Byron set out in 1764 to look for Terra Australis but accomplished little more than to arouse further enthusiasm at home. Two other British naval officers, Samuel Wallis and Philip Carteret, on the same expedition in 1767 but traveling by separate routes, made discoveries in the Tuamotus, Societies, Santa Cruz and Solomon Islands. Wallis has the credit of discovering Tahiti. He also found Rongerik in the northern Marshalls. The French explorer, Bougainville, who left his name to one of the Solomon Islands, also discovered several atolls in the Tuamotus in 1768. One of the loveliest flowers of the tropical Pacific, bougainvillea, preserves his memory.

CAPTAIN COOK'S DISCOVERIES

Captain James Cook's purpose in his first trip to the Pacific was to make a study of the Transit of Venus from the Pacific to correlate with sightings in the northern hemisphere. His orders directed him to explore the Pacific en route homeward, especially for the mythical southern continent. By the time of Cook's voyages, ships and navigational instruments both had been greatly improved. Longitude as well as latitude could be determined much more accurately than ever before. One of Cook's major contributions was to correct

[1] W. P. Morrell, *Britain in the Pacific Islands,* Oxford University Press, 1960.

the erroneous locations of numerous islands made by preceding explorers, as well as to show the nonexistence of land in places believed to have land. A score of new discoveries of islands in many parts of the south and north Pacific were also made by him. He discovered seven islands on his first trip, all in eastern Polynesia. On this trip he also circumnavigated New Zealand and defined the eastern coast of Australia. His second trip was from the west across the Indian Ocean to New Zealand and then eastward and northward to the Tuamotus, where he found additional atolls. Cook made two great counterclockwise circular sweeps of the South Pacific and proved to the world that no great continent in the south existed in habitable latitudes. On neither of the first two voyages did Cook sail north across the Equator. On the second cruise he discovered at least nineteen islands in Polynesia and Melanesia, including such important islands as the New Hebrides group and New Caledonia.

Cook's third voyage between 1776 and 1780 has come to be especially significant to the United States, since he and his successor Captain Clerke discovered the Hawaiian Islands and charted accurately for the first time the British Columbian and Alaskan coast. On his trip northward from New Zealand he also found several of the Cook Islands, Tubuai, and four islands of eastern Tonga. The completion of Cook's career, unfortunately ended by a Hawaiian spear, found the chief questions pertaining to the Pacific solved and most of the important island groups correctly located on charts.

OTHER VOYAGERS

There remained many scores of islands undiscovered to the modern world, and the British followers of Cook took their share of the honors. Captains Gilbert and Marshall in 1788 discovered many of the islands in the groups bearing their names. William Bligh of the *Bounty* in the following year discovered many of the Fiji islands, including Viti Levu, the most important, on which the present capital of Suva is located. In 1792 he returned to find five more islands in the Fijis. Five years after this, James Wilson of the British ship *Duff* discovered islands in the Tuamotus, Fijis, and Western Carolines.

Mariners of other nationalities became prominent in the history of explorers during the nineteenth century, including such Russians as Lisianski, Kotzebue, Bellingshausen, and Lütke, such Frenchmen as Duperrey and D'Urville, and various American whaling captains, as well as the Englishman Beechey, who in 1826 added four more Tuamotu atolls to the list of known islands.

The discovery of the many Pacific islands spread over vast ocean spaces sometimes occurred because of specific search, but was commonly the result of accident. Many diverse motives urged on the European and American mariners who participated in the discoveries: the search for treasure, for new dominions, for spices and rare products to seize, barter or buy, for whales to catch, for labor to enslave, and for heathen to save.

As long as geographic knowledge was uncertain, competitive claims remained subdued. With the onset of the industrial revolution, the shrinkage of the world before the advance of maritime communications, and the more accurate and widespread knowledge of Pacific geography, international competition for dominion sharpened. Increased knowledge of a vast non-Christian world also led to an era of vigorous Christian proselyting in the Pacific, with its own bitter rivalries of faiths and sects. All of these found expression in the ensuing nineteenth century.

IV *God and Mammon in the Pacific*

WESTERN civilization burst upon the Pacific islanders in the form of whalers, traders, planters, missionaries, empire builders and the many alien ideas introduced by them. Of these the new concepts brought by the missionaries had the most profound influence in changing the cultural heritage of the Pacific islanders. The bewildering differences of outlook, ethics, beliefs, and practices that were brought by different professional groups from Europe and the Americas added to the confusion following disenchantment in the native gods and taboo systems when these provided no aid in stopping the invaders. The whalers were a rough, tough lot who brought liquor, demanded native women, and transmitted disease. They paid no attention to native social organization and customs, violated taboos and helped to reduce the prestige of the chiefs. The traders took advantage of the naiveté of the natives—their craving for the wonderful and superior products of more advanced technologies and their indifference to the morrow when credit comes due—creating demands for products for which the natives were ill-prepared to pay. These products led to the decline of native skills and crafts and the dependence upon imports and the limited and vulnerable export mediums.

The planters and slave-runners developed "black-birding" and labor abuses, appropriated land by fair means and foul and created social dislocations. But it must also be said that both trader and planter stimulated economic development, the planting of coconuts and other economic plants on numerous islands and areas which had hitherto had none, and the development of a stronger discipline for work. The missionaries disrupted the old social system even more: in fact they replaced it with a completely different one not always good in every respect but, on the whole, meeting with desirable results. They succeeded in stopping widespread infanticide and barbarous practices especially inflicted upon women, in abolishing intertribe and interclan warfare, in bringing in modern medicines and medical care, in introducing education and devising written languages and in seeking to halt the abuses inflicted by unscrupulous traders, whalers and adventurers. At times, however, some of the fanatical and small-souled missionaries also contributed to the warfare, dissension, and oppression among the native peoples, although the good they did far outweighs the evil, which gets a greater amount of publicity among the novel-reading public. Finally the empire builders, whether in missionary or commercial body or in naval and civil commands, brought new and generally better codes of law, with regularized policing and judicial systems, concepts of legislative organizations and functions. In some areas this meant a welding of numerous hetero-political tribal units into larger units and ultimately even political states as in Tonga, Hawaii and now Samoa. On the other hand, the empire builders brought with them the international jealousies and power struggles of their continental homelands and, partitioning the Pacific among themselves, they took control of the islands' political destinies.

INDIGENOUS RELIGIOUS ELEMENTS

Several aspects of the early indigenous religious systems must be noted. First, much of the emphases and the sanctions were based upon a system of taboos the violation of which brought down or was supposed to bring down upon the guilty one the anger of the gods or of malevolent spirits. Since the taboos secured the superior social system of the chiefs and priests versus the common people, or the males versus the females, the beneficiary classes were vigilant in seeing that severe punishment was indeed visited upon violators, even though, at times, belief in the thought of doom was so strong that an islander would give up the will to live, stop eating, and simply die for no other good reason. A second aspect was the strength of the chiefly and communal system and the way in which the people looked to the chiefs for leadership.

Both of these elements were of great importance in determining the sudden changeover from the old religious-social systems to the new Christianity-oriented systems. The incoming Europeans demonstrated that they were not subject to the power of the taboos, that they could defy them with impunity and that they possessed in their guns, ships, equipment and accouterments, powers explicable only in terms of superior "mana" from a greater god than those of the natives. The incentive to worship gods among the islanders was, especially, the material advantages to be obtained therefrom. And the material advantages bestowed by the god of the European and American invaders were, after all, easily observable in their superior products. Thus the overthrow of the taboo system was characterized by a sudden breakdown of the old order and the sudden switch-over to the new. Conversions to Christianity were marked by wholesale landslides of the tribal or clan group to the new system when chiefs made the decision for Christianity. Nevertheless, hostility of the chiefs generally presented almost insurmountable obstacles to the missionaries. In Polynesia, especially, the priestly *ariki* often were sacred as well as chiefly, and the destruction of faith in their sacred character led to a reduction in their political and social power over their people, so they often were hostile to the missionaries. The latter, therefore, devoted special attention to the conversion of the chiefs.

In the Marshalls and Carolines there was a totemic type of religio-social system. Deified ghosts of famous people and ancestor-heroes were believed to be reincarnated in a tree, bird, fish or stone. Thus, on Ulithi Atoll, the taro plant had been the major totem. These ghosts were looked on as resident guardians and were worshipped through the intermediaries of priests. In addition there was a variety of good and evil nature-spirits to whom were attributed diseases, accidents and misfortunes and who were feared. A class of sorcerers dealt with propitiating and neutralizing these evil spirits. The religious system was clannish and not individualistic, and because of the close ties between the social structure and the religious system, the destruction of the old religious structure also meant the disintegration of the old social system.

CHRISTIAN RIVALRY AND DEMANDS

Unfortunately for the native Pacific islanders and to their confusion, there often appeared to be more than one Christian God. In Polynesia at least two European religions were bitterly hostile to each other, each declaring the teachings of the other erroneous, bad and contemptible. Each fought the other openly and secretly with chicanery, banishments, arrests and, finally, with appeals to the political power of their states. These two opposing camps were the Roman Catholic and the Protestant faiths. As if this were not confusing enough, such a varying array of sects as the Mormons, Seventh-Day Adventists, Wesleyans, and the London Missionary Society tried to establish spheres of evangelicalism from which each tried to exclude other faiths. Whatever the muddle of conflicting religious faiths, all the missionaries were in the position of protectors of the natives from the demoralizing influences of whalers, traders, adventurers or beachcombers, who naturally fought against the restrictions placed upon them by the missionaries. Many of the native chiefs and their subjects also resented interference with their acquisitions of liquor, tobacco, guns and other weapons, or with the prostitution of their women to further such purposes. The discipline exacted by the British and American Protestant missionaries upon their converts was often very demanding. This was less so among the Catholic missionaries who, although demanding submissiveness in all that the Church required at home, showed more tolerance to inherited traditions and practices and were more lax in rules of dress and Sabbath, the use of tobacco, liquor and the like. This gave the Catholics a distinct advantage in attracting adherents.

Among the Protestants, Sunday church activities became the pivot around which community social life revolved. Observance of the Holy Day was strict. All work became taboo, even the making of fires and preparing of meals, so that the food had to be prepared on Saturday. Clothing covering the female body was believed needed to effectively combat immorality. In some areas the policing of the community by church elders went to extreme lengths. Violations of the Sabbath at Tahiti and other places were punished by inflicting work-penalties in road construction. On the other hand, the punishments for breaches of social and religious rules and regulations were much more lenient than those inflicted by the old society for breaches of taboo. Although today such penalties are no longer inflicted, some of the Christian religious practices of the earlier period are so deeply ingrained that on many islands, for instance, any kind of work on Sunday meets strong social disapproval, and among Protestant groups church members may not smoke or drink alcoholic drinks.

Church and state have been most closely linked in those island groups where control came into Spanish or French hands, and these links reflect the predominantly Roman Catholic religion of the homeland. Although both Protestant and Catholic missionaries called for naval and military backing for their proselyting efforts at times, such forces were most often and consistently exerted by the Catholic powers. Undeniably, this has been important in the present prevalence of Roman Catholicism throughout the areas where the Spanish were in most constant control, as in the Marianas, Yap and Palaus (as well as in the Philippines), and in the various parts of French Oceania.

By contrast, areas that came under British, German or American control, although most affected by Protestant influence, also were opened to a considerable degree to Roman Catholic proselyting. However, the dominance of one or the other of the religious groups or sects in the early period particularly depended upon the availability of missionaries in the different islands and island groups. There often were not enough missionaries of a particular faith to effectively monopolize a related cluster or chain of islands or even the scattered tribes of one island that might have strong cultural ties.

PROSELYTIZING IN MICRONESIA

The Marianas were the first of the central Pacific islands to be Christianized, starting with the visit of a Spanish Franciscan who disembarked in 1596 and stayed for a year. Nothing further was done, however, until 70 years later, when a Jesuit priest accompanied by a small unit of about 30 soldiers and two officers began in 1668 a successful conversion of the Chamoros of Guam. Periodic uprisings by people of the Mariana islands between 1670 and 1695 resulted in Spanish military pacification and the forced movement of their populations to concentrate upon the single island of Guam. The Jesuits were later followed by the Augustinians, then by the fathers of the Capuchin Order. Protestant missionaries have at no time been active in the Marianas.

The economic development of the Marianas progressed very little during the Spanish period. The natives exchanged food products such as rice, yams, bananas, coconuts and fish for much coveted objects of iron. Until 1828 the governor monopolized the trade, selling the products from his store at high prices. Some improvement in the economy followed the Spanish introduction of cattle, pigs, goats, deer, poultry, tobacco, corn, sweet potatoes, coffee and cacao. Unlike elsewhere in the Central Pacific, the coming of the whalers in the early 19th century produced no important adverse effects upon the native people here, since European diseases had long ago killed off the most susceptible, and the Spanish authorities already were well established in political and civil control.

Missionary influence in the Carolines began relatively much later than in the Marianas. In the Western Carolines early Spanish missionary activities were withdrawn following the murder of a Jesuit father at Ulithi Atoll in 1773. The much later work of Roman Catholic priests in Yap (beginning in 1885) and the Palau (beginning in 1891) has made half the population Catholic in religion. In the rest of the Carolines and in the Marshalls, Americans of the Hawaiian Evangelical Mission were the first to work, beginning in Ponape and Kusaie in 1852 and at Ebon in the southern Marshalls and Abaiang in the northern Gilberts in 1857. Their work was extended to Tarawa in 1858. In the Marshalls and Gilberts Protestantism obtained the firmest hold, the Marshallese being overwhelmingly the spiritual offspring of the Boston Congregationalists through their Hawaiian Mission. In the Carolines as a whole, however, the religious history is much more bound up with the power politics of the area and will be discussed further in some later paragraphs.

CHRISTIANIZATION OF POLYNESIA

English missionaries arrived in Polynesia in the last years of the 18th century. Their success in the Societies was retarded by the introduction of ravaging diseases which were blamed upon them. Their involvement in local tribal wars in Tonga led to the abandonment of Tonga by the London Missionary Society, but Wesleyan Methodists took up the work in 1822. The conversion of Chief Pomare in Tahiti and his forgiveness of his enemies brought a stop to the local wars and caused the rise of the chief to supreme power. The cessation of human sacrifices and infanticide accompanied the destruction of the old sacred *maraes* (shrines or ritual sites) and images, and the institution of strict church observances. The missionaries in 1891 prepared a code of laws for this realm and were influential in reducing the severity of the penal code. Tahitian converts spread the desire for Christianity to the Tuamotus, Cook and other island groups in the area. Missionary authority on some of the Cook Islands became so strong as to supercede that of the chiefs, and virtual Christian theocracies came into existence. In Tonga, the conversion of chief Joseph Tupou was the beginning of change to Christianity. Samoa came more easily into the Christian fold. Indeed, one chief tried to monopolize it for his own followers. Other chiefs, however, appealed to the Tonga Wesleyans for religious teachers. In order to avoid conflict, an agreement between the London Missionary Society and the Wesleyans divided the work so that the former took responsibility for Tonga and the latter for the Fijis.

The first political intervention occasioned by religion occurred when certain French Catholic priests decided that Catholicism should not stand by without counter effort when, according to Roman dogma, Protestants were leading the heathen astray from the true faith. They attempted to gain a foothold on Mangareva where laws supported by the London Missionaries forbade the landing of strangers without the chief's consent. Their expulsion from this island, followed by similar expulsions from Tahiti and the Hawaiian

Islands, brought about their appeal for official French backing. A French warship was sent to both Tahiti and Hawaii with an ultimatum demanding and getting indemnities as well as equal rights with Protestants. It is possible that a more liberal Protestant position at Tahiti might have saved a larger field for Protestant endeavor and prevented its acquisition by the French. Today the Society Islanders are mostly Catholic, with the remainder being largely Mormons and Seventh Day Adventists. The early successes of the London Missionaries were rapidly lost.

In Hawaii, the first missionaries to arrive came from Boston in 1820, and the Boston missionaries and their heirs came to exercise a remarkable influence and power politically and economically, as well as religiously, in the life of the Hawaiian Islands.

MISSIONARIES IN MELANESIA

Farther west in New Caledonia, the French Roman Catholics were successful in gaining adherents in 1843 when they began their work. In the Solomons, British Protestant missionary efforts began in the 1840's but made little progress during the next 25 years. Here, even more than elsewhere, the multiplicity of languages and the numerous islands and interisland conflicts were retarding influences. Tribal chiefs here were less influential than in the Fijis, where the patronage and conversion of leading chiefs made for the success of the missions.

CONFLICTING FAITHS

In general, the pattern of Christian religious persuasions in Polynesia, Micronesia and eastern Melanesia was firmly established during the 19th century, and most of the peoples of these areas belong to one or another of the different Christian faiths or sects. The existence of competing sects or faiths upon individual small islands has had unfortunate effects in dividing once closely knit community groups. Perplexing problems arise in such matters as traditional community use-rights, ownership of properties, or in traditional cooperative work activities.

V *The Political Division of the Pacific*

ALTHOUGH the act of discovery of an island or group of islands gives the discoverers a basis for first claims to their discovery, sovereignty comes only with effective occupation and annexation or the establishment of a protectorate. The discoverers did not always lay claims for their discoveries, nor were the European nations always eager for the responsibilities on Pacific islands that devolved upon political sovereigns. These responsibilities included the establishment of a system of law and the protection not only of one's own nationals, but also of foreign visitors, missionaries and traders, and of the native population from lawless and rebellious elements. If the influential tribes or chiefs did not all agree to come under such rule, there also were the problems of pacification of dissident groups. All of these measures were costly and were disliked by home tax-payers. Moreover, as long as no single nation decided to annex islands in one area, the other nations theoretically had equal rights and would not set up rival domains. The determination by one nation to establish sovereignty over one area immediately aroused jealous protests or produced counter claims or annexations elsewhere. Thus, although Great Britain had on numerous occasions opportunities to annex groups of islands and was even petitioned to do so by the leading chiefs or by her nationals, whether missionaries or traders, she was extremely reluctant to initiate sovereignty proceedings.

The causes leading to annexations were varied. They included political backing for religious or commercial groups desiring effective protection against hostile acts of natives or other foreign nationals, the desire of native chiefs fearing annexation by unwanted powers or wishing thereby to gain power over rival chiefs, the maneuvering of traders, planters or guano exploiters wishing to establish pre-eminent economic domains, the desire of navies to establish naval and coaling stations, or the wish of a state to secure an island for a transoceanic cable station—all of these motives have been operative at one time or another.

FRANCE ACQUIRES THE MARQUESAS AND SOCIETIES

In the Marquesas the French Catholics were successful in 1838 in establishing a mission where the London Missionaries failed. When Chief Iotete plundered an American whaler and feared retaliation, he sought protection from a French naval commander. The latter agreed to provide this only when Iotete signed a document accepting French sovereignty on May 1, 1842. Following the expulsion of French Catholic priests from Tahiti and Hawaii, the French officer Du Petit-Thouars stampeded Queen Pomare of Tahiti with an ultimatum into signing the cession of her domain. The Frenchman thereupon proclaimed a protectorate. British authorities refused to accept this. In negotiations, the home governments of these two nations agreed that the French should retain Tahiti, and France would recognize the cession of Hawaii to Great Britain.

HAWAII BECOMES AMERICAN

Although the Hawaiian chiefs appeared quite agreeable to this course, United States interests became aroused, and the American Government announced its paramount interests in the Hawaiian Islands and its strong opposition to British annexation. Since the British had proclaimed eminant domain in New Zealand, Britain felt that it could not deny the French insistence on a protectorate in the Societies even though it did not annex Hawaii. Instead Hawaii was recognized as a neutral zone under its native Polynesian dynasty. American interests and influence here steadily increased. In 1893 the reigning queen Liliuokalani was deposed by a revolution and a republic was set up under the presidency of Sanford B. Dole immortalized in the pineapple industry of Hawaii. Five years later, the island legislature requested annexation by the United States. This was accomplished in the same year, on August 12, 1898.

THE BRITISH GAIN THE FIJIS

The British annexation of the Fijis resulted more from politics and civil strife within these islands rather than from external international politics. As early as 1858 the leading chief Thakombau announced the cession of the Fijis to Britain. However, he ruled over only a part of the area and had no authority for the whole area. His action was precipitated by fear that the American commercial agent in the Fijis was going to obtain the backing of an American warship to seize and deport him because of some unjustly large debts claimed against him. Britain refused the importunities of the British Consul Pritchard, however. On the other hand, the Americans soon got too involved with the Civil War in their homeland to act on the pleas of resident Americans in the Fijis. Similar pleas by German commercial interests to their home government aroused among the Australians the fear of German annexation. Australia passed a resolution asserting that no country other than Great Britain should have the protectorate. The British finally agreed when in 1874 all the important chiefs signed an unconditional petition for annexation. Rotuma was similarly annexed in 1881. In this same year France formally annexed Tahiti, and in 1887 she extended annexation to the rest of the Societies and the Tuamotus without British objection.

THE DIVISION OF THE SAMOAS

As a result of the commercial activities of the German firm of J. C. Godeffroy and Son, Samoa became the major trading center among the Pacific islands during the 1860's. The German navy also thought Samoa would make a good stop for its warships traveling between Tsingtao in China and the Atlantic. Its central position also favored it as a crossroads between Hawaii and New Zealand

and between the Societies and the islands of Micronesia and Melanesia. Rival commercial agents and rival mission work among Anglicans, Methodists and Roman Catholics, however, kept the native communities in the group from attaining political unity.

Until after the Civil War in the United States, American interests were not as important as those of the Germans and the British. However, in 1871 W. H. Webb, an American ship-builder, developed a regular steamship service to New Zealand. In the following year the chief of Tutuila Island signed over exclusive use of the fine harbor of Pago Pago to the United States for a naval station, following which various Samoan chiefs petitioned for annexation by the United States. New Zealanders also urged Great Britain to establish a protectorate to forestall the Germans, who were making separate commercial treaties with the Samoan and Fijian chiefs. The consuls for all three major powers were concluding conflicting agreements. In an attempt to present a *fait accompli,* the Germans with a show of naval force in 1887 installed a chief favorable to them as king of Samoa and exiled the previous king Malietoa to Jaluit in the Marshalls. A German was also made premier of Samoa. The revolt by the Samoans and the outspoken opposition of the United States dissolved this German-installed regime. A "neutral" government was then installed by tripartite agreement through the institution of a Swedish-appointed chief justice to supervise a Samoan regime.

The subsequent division of Samoa resulted from the rivalry of German and British interests in the Solomons, the Bismarcks and the eastern half of New Guinea. The Australians were particularly aroused by the lack of British action to stop the German advance here which resulted in German annexation of northeastern New Guinea and New Britain in 1884. Only a typhoon stopped a naval conflict between German and U.S. warships in Samoa in 1889. To settle the difficulties the tripartite agreement on Samoa was changed in 1897. Eastern Samoa was ceded to the United States. Great Britain gave up her rights in Western Samoa to the Germans in return for German concessions in western Melanesia in favor of the British.

MELANESIAN SPOILS

East and south of the Solomons the New Caledonia French were involved in conflicts with the British Australians over New Hebrides and the Santa Cruz Islands. A mixed Anglo-French naval commission was arranged in 1887 to exercise condominion rule over the New Hebrides, and the Santa Cruz Islands became British.

THE GUANO ISLANDS

As a result of the Guano Act passed by the United States Congress in 1856, Americans discovering unoccupied guano islands were authorized to claim them. Both British and American interests were active in claiming and exploiting guano islands. These were especially numerous in the dry Line Islands, and also on Ocean and Nauru. Guano companies introduced coconut plantations where rainfall was sufficient to permit them.

GERMAN-SPANISH CLAIMS

Although Spain had vague claims to all of Micronesia, she showed little interest in the eastern groups such as the Gilberts and the Marshalls. The Germans thus met little opposition in extending their trading activities in the Marshalls. Here the firm of Hernsheim gained dominance and made Jaluit their headquarters. A German naval captain in 1878 got the Jaluit islanders to cede the island to Germany as a coaling station. Seven years later this was followed by the establishment of a German protectorate over all of the Marshalls.

In the Carolines, which the Germans attempted to take over in the same year, Spain disputed the claim. The Germans did not want to alienate their Spanish friends, and the two nations submitted the dispute to arbitration by the Pope. The papal award gave sovereignty to Spain but gave equal trade, navigation, fishery, and plantation rights to both, as well as the right to a naval base to Germany.

THE GILBERTS, ELLICES, COOK'S

In the following year, 1886, an Anglo-German convention agreed to British control over the Gilberts. The problems of administering a group of 16 islands having 13 different native "governments" made the British reluctant to establish a protectorate. However, fear of possible German action brought formal annexation proclamations in 1892 over the Gilberts and over the Ellices, whose islanders asked also to be annexed. In the Cook Islands and the atolls to their north, fear of French action already had made these British in 1888. The discovery of phosphate on Ocean brought quick annexation by Great Britain in 1900.

THE UNITED STATES ACQUIRES GUAM

The final drama of the 19th century division of the Pacific came with the American victory in the Spanish-American war. An unfortunate lack of insight into the strategic importance of Micronesia by the American Government led to the loss of the opportunity for the United States to acquire the Marianas and the Carolines at that time. The United States contented itself with Guam in the peace settlement in 1898. Spain, in financial difficulties and finding the islands of no economic profit, sold her remaining Marianas and the Carolines to Germany in the next year for $4,500,000. However, the political history of the Carolines has been so turbulent as to warrant more than such a summary account.

CLASHES ON PONAPE

The political pattern of the Carolines has always been intricate and diverse. Kusaie in the east was the best organized under the rule of a single king. Ponape, a much larger and more populous island, had five separate kings, and it and its surrounding islands were better organized than the communities at Truk and in the low islands to its west. Yap was the seat of a trading empire among the low islands of the West Carolines including areas as far east as Puluwat. There was no political unity in the whole area, of course. On the contrary, on most of the individual islands there was a strong feeling of separateness and virtually no feeling of a common nationality.

Protestant Christian missionary work in the Carolines began in 1852 on Ponape and Kusaie, but some Western acculturation preceded this. Numerous whaling ships had been making visits in these islands since the first two decades of the 19th century. The mission success was most spectacular in Kusaie where the Christianized commoners deposed the pagan king in 1874 and elected a Christian to the office. At Ponape things progressed much more slowly and unevenly, and the entry of a Spanish military administration bringing with it a Roman Catholic Mission created an explosive situation.

Although Spain claimed the Carolines, she did not establish direct administration here until the German empire building threatened to appropriate the Carolines along with the Marshalls. Following the papal award of the Carolines to Spain, the Spanish military in the Philippines despatched a small force with a governor accompanied by some Catholic priests to Ponape, which became the administrative center for the Eastern Carolines. Spanish ineptness brought on insurrections by the natives supported in part by the American Protestant missionaries. Despite military campaigns and the expulsion of the American missionaries by the Spaniards, the Spanish were unable to pacify the island. Armed clashes continued to occur between the natives and the Spaniards until the end of their rule in 1899, when Germany bought the Carolines. The native peoples, needless to say, were not consulted, nor had they any say in this transaction.

GERMAN ADMINISTRATION OF MICRONESIA

The unsuccessful Spanish pacification measures no doubt encouraged the Ponapean view that the Germans could be defied as well, and sporadic insurrections continued until 1911 when a more vigorous German campaign brought defeat to the rebels, on this occasion largely from Jokaj district in the northwest section of

Ponape. The Jokaj inhabitants were exiled en mass to Palau and Yap and their homelands given to immigrant communities brought in from overpopulated low atolls in the Ponape region. The futility of insurrection against the much superior political and military organizations of European powers was finally brought home to the Ponapeans, and overt armed rebellions in the Carolines ceased from then on.

The Germans conducted a firm and modernized administration in Micronesia which on the whole could be described as successful. In contrast to the Spanish, whose Pacific rule was characterized by a predominantly Catholic religious interest, the Germans made trade and commerce their goal. Under the German administration Jaluit became the administrative center for the Marshalls, Ponape for the Eastern Carolines and Yap for the Western Carolines. Yap was the early headquarters for the leading German firms of Godeffroy, Capelle and Hernsheim. The Germans beginning in 1904 also made Yap the center for an important Pacific cable network. German cables led from Yap to Guam, from Yap to Shanghai and from Yap to Celebes. Other lines connected the Philippines and points in Asia to Yap, which became the nerve center for West Pacific cable communications. Yap thus became prominent in American considerations at a time when the outbreak of World War I destroyed the German empire in the Pacific and spread over it the flag of the Rising Sun.

THE JAPANESE MANDATES

The decision of Japan to enter World War I on the side of the Allies against the Imperial Powers was not made because Japan at this time had developed any great enmity toward Germany, but rather because she found that this fitted in very neatly with her evolving plans for empire expansion. Although she was, of course, in alliance with Great Britain, there was a price tag for her support in ousting Germany from the Pacific and providing shipping to aid the Allied cause. This price included French, Russian, and British support for her taking German Micronesia. The secret character of the agreement presented the United States with a *fait accompli* at the Versailles Conference. The League of Nations therefore was able to do little more than attach some restrictions in confirming a Mandate of German Micronesia upon Japan. These included the obligation to promote the material and moral welfare of the native islanders and Japan's agreement not to develop military fortifications in the islands concerned. The United States also demanded equal rights of access to Yap with its trans-Pacific cables. The grudging concession to this in words by Japan after a bitter year of dispute did not produce such equality in practice.

Japan was not the only power gaining former German territory. New Zealand was given a Mandate over Western Samoa by the League, and Australia was similarly awarded Mandates over northeastern New Guinea, the Bismarcks, the northern Solomons and the phosphate island of Nauru, all of which had been former German possessions or protectorates. The most marked difference between Japan's role in Micronesia and those of the Germans and Spanish is that Japanese settlers moved in in large numbers on the larger islands of the Carolines and Marianas—especially Saipan, Tinian, the Palaus, Truk and Ponape, and even Jaliut among the Marshalls atolls.

JAPAN'S STRATEGIC PREPARATIONS

Micronesia was governed by a civil administration from 1922 until Japan's withdrawal from the League in 1935. Japan was embarking upon her expansion on the China mainland at this time, and her admirals looked upon the Pacific island possessions as a military screen protecting her in the event of future war with other Pacific powers. A cloak of secrecy was thrown over her Micronesian islands and she began to fortify selected islands. Of these Truk in the central Carolines was thought to be the most impregnable at a time when military aircraft had not yet been developed to its subsequent potent state. Military, airforce and naval bases also were ultimately constructed in such areas as Saipan, Tinian, the Palaus and Yap in the west, and in the east in Ponape, Jaluit, Kwajalein, Eniwetok, Wotje and Maloelap.

It is obvious that Japan had worked out a careful timetable of military preparation leading up to the sudden surprise attack upon Pearl Harbor December 7, 1941. Her Micronesian stepping stones reached two thousand miles southward and southeastward into the west-central Pacific. She had fortified air and naval bases in the near north and south of the United States base at Guam. She reached southwestward in the Ryukyus and Taiwan to within about 250 miles of Luzon, while her bases in the Palaus were only about 600 miles from Davao in Mindanao in the southern Philippines. From Jaluit, her naval forces were within about 250 miles of Tarawa in the Gilberts. At Truk Japanese air and naval forces were only about 600 miles from the Bismarck Archipelago and the fine naval harbor of Rabaul. In the far north of the Kuriles, acquired by trade with the Russians in exchange for giving up Japanese claims to Sakhalin Island in 1873, Japan's powerful naval base on Paramushiro brought her harbored ships within some 750 miles of American Attu at the end of the Aleutian chain. Such was her strategic situation in the Pacific when she decided to make her bid for undisputed dominance in the Pacific.

JAPAN'S MISCALCULATION

Although Japan's surprise attack gave her temporary strategic advantages, it did not provide her the time within which her militarists thought they could consolidate their Asiatic conquests. They were unprepared for the tremendous organizational drive, the latent industrial capacity and labor power, the ingenuity, the reservoir of patriotic spirit, and the willingness to work and to sacrifice that belie the softness attributed to a people so richly endowed as the motley North Americans. Inexorably, the vast concentration of power marshalled by the Americans and their Allies in the Pacific wiped out or isolated the Japanese armies scattered over the Pacific, sank their fleets and destroyed their air forces. The Japanese surrender, signed August 19, 1945, ended the major agony on both sides that had lasted three years, eight months, and 26 days.

VI *The Pacific War 1941-1945*

THE attack on Pearl Harbor on December 7, 1941 was followed by an immediate push by the Japanese to occupy islands farthest east and south. By the end of the year Guam, Wake and the Gilberts, as well as the Philippines, were in Japanese hands. While the United States gradually recovered her strength in the early part of 1942, the Japanese drove on to occupy the western Aleutians as far east as Kiska. In the south Japanese military and naval forces pushed into and occupied the Netherlands empire in Indonesia as well as northeastern New Guinea, the Bismarcks and the Solomons as far south as Guadalcanal. By August 7, 1942, she had extended herself as far as she was to be able to go.

In the Central Pacific, after the battle of Midway, Japanese military forces adopted a strictly defensive strategy, attempting to consolidate their gains thereafter. Japanese armies were spread over an enormous area, and the fleet units had to be grouped into smaller task forces to safeguard land areas exposed to potential attack. Mahan's strategic principles of concentration and attack were thereby ignored. Japanese military consolidation was based upon the belief that land-based planes could cause such heavy losses to attacking forces that the remnants could easily be destroyed by nearby naval task forces.

JAPANESE DEFENSIVE BASES

Three concentric lines of defense formed the framework protecting the farflung Japanese oceanic empire. Her inner line stretched from her home islands through the Ryukyus to Taiwan, through Korea to China's coasts, and through the Kuriles to Kamchatka.

A second line ran from the Bonins through the Marianas and Guam to Truk, Palau, the Philippines, and South China. The outer defenses stretched from the Aleutians through Wake Island, the Marshalls, Gilberts, Solomons, Indonesia and the Southeast Asian mainland adjoining Singapore. Key strongholds in the intermediate line were Saipan, Truk and Manila. In the outer line were Kwajalein, Rabaul, Surabaya, and Singapore. A string of closely linked and mutually supported airfields in the central and west Pacific islands convinced Japanese strategists that they could make an American advance across the ocean prohibitively costly. The fallacy of their calculations was soon demonstrated when it was shown that fleets with enough carrier force air-cover could go where they pleased.

THE AMERICAN ATTACK

Beginning as early as February 1, 1942, American carriers and cruisers inflicted severe bombardment upon Japanese fortifications, ships and men upon the atolls of Wotje, Maloelap, Kwajalein, and Jaluit in the Marshalls, and upon Makin in the Gilberts. Wake was raided on February 24. In the far south, Lae and Salamaua on New Guinea were attacked by American, Australian, and New Zealand forces on March 10, while the first strike on Tokyo was carried out on April 18. On May 7-8, the naval battle of the Coral Sea shut off the Japanese from further southward advance, while the battle of Midway during June 3-6 produced a calamitous effect upon Japan's air and carrier forces.

The campaign for the Solomons began on August 7, 1942, and the Japanese were forced to evacuate Guadalcanal during February 7-8 of the following year. Australian and American land forces under General MacArthur fought their way through the islands northwestward and along the coast of New Guinea. In March the Japanese felt the punch of the American navy off the Komandorskie Islands near the Aleutians. By the latter part of May a two week campaign brought the American reoccupation of Attu. This was followed by the reoccupation of Kiska on August 15. Such wide ranging action would appear to indicate that the Americans, also, had forgotten Mahan's principle of concentration. However, the Americans possessed the qualification that justified the exception to the rule—overwhelming superiority of striking power.

AMERICAN STRATEGIES

Actually, the three United States services differed as to the best strategy upon which to concentrate. The Army believed that assault upon the home islands of Japan would be needed to bring Japanese surrender. This strategy required recapture of the Philippines and of Okinawa as rear and forward staging bases. The Naval admirals believed that by cutting off supply lines, especially to Indonesia's oil, and by destruction of the enemy fleet, Japan could be blockaded and starved into submission. The seizure of Luzon or Formosa might accomplish this, or even the capture of the Marianas and the interception of supply vessels from bases there. The Air Force generals, for the most part, felt that bombardment of Japanese industries in the home islands by airplanes based upon the Marianas and perhaps also upon Okinawa was the quickest and cheapest way to end the war, and therefore they advocated the capture of these islands.

It was fortunate for the United States that the outstanding superiority of American military and industrial resources permitted a strategy that combined all three viewpoints. A plan of dual advance toward the Philippines was chosen by the Joint Chiefs of Staff. One line of advance was followed by the Fifth Fleet striking through the Central Pacific from Pearl Harbor, now again a mighty fortress, but an alert one. The Southwest Pacific line of advance moved northwest from the Solomons, bypassing Truk, which was neutralized by air bombardment. Both lines converged upon the Philippines. The Japanese militarists were kept guessing as to the next major American move, when carrier-based planes made strikes from August to October 1943 upon Wake and Marcus in the Central Pacific, and upon Tarawa and Abemama in the Gilberts to the south. Tarawa, with some 3500 Japanese troops, was heavily fortified and, together with the Marshalls, had to be taken to protect the American flank in the westward advance.

THE BATTLE OF TARAWA

While American attacks upon the Japanese forces at Rabaul and Bougainville were in progress during early November 1943, preparations were made to capture the Gilberts. The initial landing on Makin on November 20 met with small resistance, and Makin was captured two days later. The battle for Tarawa November 21-24 was the first experience of American armed forces in frontal assault against a well-defended reef-bound atoll. There was only one beach where a landing was possible, and the assault was unfortunately planned for a period of neap tide when it proved that landing boats could not cross the reef. In spite of heavy bombardment over a period of weeks and immediately preceding the landing, the Japanese dugouts, pillboxes and shelters remained partially intact. Although virtually the entire Japanese defending force was killed in the battle, the cost in American lives almost equalled that of the defenders and was much heavier than had been anticipated.

THE CAPTURE OF THE MARSHALLS

The Navy had learned its lesson well on Tarawa and made adequate preliminary bombardment by both aircraft and surface ships upon the Marshalls atolls that were fortified or that supported airfields. Beginning January 29, 1944, operations larger than any before were directed against the Marshalls: Kwajalein, Wotje, Mille, Jaluit, Maloelap, and Eniwetok. Wake was also bombed again. On January 31 American marines landed on Majuro but found the Japanese had withdrawn. Most of the several thousand Japanese troops on Kwajalein were killed by the bombardment, and the final assault cost the Americans fewer than 100 killed and 400 wounded. Landings were made on various islands of this atoll on February 2, and by February 8 the entire atoll was in American control. Wotje, Jaluit, Mille, and Ponape were bombed often during February. While heavy damage was being inflicted by air and naval bom-

TIDES of WAR in the PACIFIC

U.S.S.R.
KAMCHATKA PENINSULA
ATTU
KISKA
ALEUTIAN ISLANDS
MANCHURIA
KURIL ISLANDS
NORTH PACIFIC OCEAN
JAPAN
Tokyo
CHINA
BONIN IS.
MARCUS I.
PHILIPPINE ISLANDS
WAKE
MARIANA IS.
SAIPAN
TINIAN
GUAM
ENIWETOK
KWAJALEIN
CAROLINE IS.
TRUK
MARSHALL IS.
PALAU IS.
GILBERT IS.
TARAWA
NEW GUINEA
EAST INDIES
SOLOMON ISLANDS
SOUTH PACIFIC OCEAN
Darwin
CORAL SEA
GUADALCANAL
NEW HEBRIDES
FIJI IS.
AUSTRALIA
HANKINS

LEGEND

Japanese Position Prior to Dec. 7, 1941
Japanese Aggression, Dec 7, 1941 - Jan. 1, 1942
Japanese Aggression, Jan. 1, 1942 - Aug 7, 1942
Status - Dec. 31, 1943
Status - Feb. 29, 1944

bardment upon Truk on February 17-18, a landing was effected upon Eniwetok after several days of bombardment. The capture of the entire atoll on February 20, 1944, marked the complete destruction of the Japanese forces in the Marshalls.

THE BATTLES FOR GUAM AND THE MARIANAS

During the first few months of 1944, some of the most difficult operations of the war were being carried on for the capture of the Bismarcks, the Admiralties and New Guinea. These operations were wound up with the final drive in July of 1944 on the Vogelkop peninsula of northwest New Guinea where some 18,000 Japanese troops were caught unprepared. MacArthur's headquarters was moved from Australia to Hollandia September 8 for the drive on the Philippines.

On February 23 heavy raids were made upon Saipan, Guam and Tinian in the Central Pacific line of advance. The capture of the Marianas would open the way to assault upon Japan's inner line of defense. The thrust from Tarawa to Kwajalein meant a 700-mile step. Eniwetok brought the Americans another 400 miles westward and to the much longer jump of 1200 miles to Guam, Saipan and Tinian. Here they faced a much more formidable assemblage of armed might than in the Marshalls and Gilberts. The 53,000 Japanese soldiers on the three islands, however, faced more than twice that many United States soldiers and marines.

Before the landings were made, warships and carrier-based planes bombarded and bombed Japanese concentrations and installations and destroyed their aircraft and the supply convoys and escorts. Mahan's principle of concentration was fully exploited in the tremendous massing of strength. Over 600 ships of all types, some 2000 planes and more than 300,000 men were involved in the Marianas operations. Attacks to neutralize Japanese bases in the Palaus, Yap and Truk preceded the landing. Despite this overwhelming superiority, the assaults, landings and subsequent battles presented serious obstacles, since the defenders were well entrenched. The

Japanese soldiers fought bravely and with a fanaticism in keeping with their battle ethics never to be taken alive. Virtually all the strictly military Japanese personnel of 30,000 on Saipan were killed in the battle, and some 3400 American soldiers and marines lost their lives, while another 11,000 Americans were wounded, before the island was taken July 9.

Additional bombings and bombardment of Guam, Tinian, and the rest of the fortified Marianas, as well as of Japanese bases in the Bonins, preceded the amphibious landing on Guam on July 21 and, two days later, on Tinian. Tinian was taken nine days later, but it was not until August 10 that organized Japanese resistance ceased on Guam. Only a few hundred of the 18,500 Japanese soldiers on Guam surived to hide in the bush and snipe at the Americans until the end of the war.

The capture of Guam and Saipan marked a major turning point in the Pacific War, for the Japanese mainland industrial centers were thus brought within range of the B-29 superfortress planes. Based upon the large airfields on these islands, these planes for the first time subjected Japanese cities to frequent massive bombing assaults. These raids ultimately resulted in the destruction of almost one third of Japan's entire capital plant.

THE CAPTURE OF PELELIU AND ANGAUR

The capture of Guam, Saipan, and Tinian provided important supply bases, and the neutralization of the rest of the Marianas and Bonins opened two routes of advance. One went northward through the Bonins directly to Japan, the other southwestward to Yap, the Palaus and the Philippines. The southern flank had to be secured before the invasion of Japan, and the next logical targets, therefore, were Yap and the Palau islands. Only Peleliu and Angaur of the seven large islands in the Palaus were actually taken. Peleliu marked one of the bloodiest battles of the island warfare. Landings were made here on September 15, followed two days later by landings on Angaur. On the latter the weak resistance was virtually ended three days later, but on Peleliu stubborn fighting continued until October 12. Since the Japanese forces on Yap and the other Palau islands were cut off from air and naval support, it was decided that they, like Truk, could be bypassed safely, while the attention now turned upon the Philippines.

THE PHILIPPINE CAMPAIGNS

The main invasion fleet for the Philippines was massed in New Guinea and the Admiralties and from there steamed 1000-1500 miles into Leyte Gulf on October 20, 1944. The Japanese rushed reinforcements from China to Ormoc Bay on the west coast of Leyte after miscalculations by General Kuroda. He had believed that the Americans would attack Luzon in two prongs instead of carrying out a major assault upon Leyte. Part of the Japanese reinforcements met with disaster when four transports and five escorting warships were sunk by American planes.

The main part of the Japanese fleet based upon Singapore decided to make a desperate attempt to regain control of the much restricted area in which it still could operate. Through a combination of mischance, miscalculation and bad strategy, the Imperial Fleet suffered an irretrievable disaster in the series of naval and air battles of Leyte Gulf and the South China Sea from October 23 to October 25. With this great defeat, the Japanese fleet was reduced to a fraction of its earlier strength. There was no hope of recovery from this blow. The campaign on Leyte ended on December 26 with the Japanese losses totaling over 113,000 men on land and sea. A further loss of 26,000 occurred in American mopping-up operations.

From Leyte the campaign moved on to Mindoro and then to Luzon where the landing was made in Lingayen Gulf on January 9. On February 15 Manila Bay was retaken. The battle for Luzon was essentially over with the capture of the Cagayan Valley by American troops and Filipino guerrillas on June 23. Thereafter, the campaign in the Philippines broke up into a series of isolated actions on the various islands.

THE BATTLE FOR IWO JIMA

The direction of the American advance now turned toward the heart of the Japanese empire. American carriers now were in a position to sail close in for air strikes at Tokyo itself, as well as at every part of the home islands of Japan. Japanese bases in the Kuriles from Paramushiro southward were being kept under attacks from the Aleutian air bases. In the Volcano Islands Iwo Jima, 650 miles from Tokyo, had three airfields that could be used by both bombers and fighter escorts. It was decided that Iwo Jima should be captured to support the final assault upon the Japanese main islands. The Japanese had constructed one of the most effective defensive organizations here. The beaches were flanked by high terrain with imbedded gun emplacements for cross-fire. 20,000 Japanese defenders fought from interlocked underground fortifications and high concealed lookout points. Over 60,000 American marines fought some of the most gallant actions of the Pacific War against equally brave and determined enemies for twenty-six days before organized resistance was declared ended on March 17. More than 4000 American marines were killed and almost 16,000 wounded in its capture.

THE BATTLE FOR OKINAWA

In the final step before the invasion of Japan itself, the Allied Forces had to destroy the Japanese inner line bases in the Ryukyu archipelago. On the chief island of Okinawa were some 120,000 Japanese soldiers with many airfields and planes. More than half a million men, 318 combat vessels and 1139 auxiliary craft were used in the assault. This started with a feint at landing on April 1 in the south where the bulk of the Japanese were massed, but the actual landing took place in the middle section of the western Peninsula. After this landing, drives were made northward and southward.

The battle for Okinawa was the costliest single operation of the Pacific War. Virtually all of the defending Japanese forces were casualties, while the attacking American and British forces suffered some 47,000 casualties, including dead and wounded. The Japanese lost over 3400 planes, while over 1000 American planes were destroyed. Some 250 Allied ships were hit by air attacks, largely from desperate suicidal kamikaze attacks, and thiry-four Allied destroyers and lesser vessels were sunk. On June 21, after eighty-two days of battle, Okinawa was in Allied hands, and the way was clear for the thrust at Kyushu and Honshu in Japan proper.

THE NUCLEAR ATTACK ENDING THE WAR

This grand assault was to have taken place in the fall of 1945, but on August 5 and August 9 atomic bombs were dropped upon Hiroshima and Nagasaki, leading to Japan's decision for unconditional surrender. On August 15 Allied offensive operations ceased with the broadcast of Emperor Hirohito's order for the cessation of all hostilities. The surrender, officially signed August 19, ended the Pacific War that had lasted three years, eight months and twenty-six days.

If the atomic bombs may be regarded as the most decisive factor leading to Japanese surrender, then statistically the nuclear attack must be regarded as a great boon not only to the Allies but also to Japan. The total casualties of Hiroshima numbered 306,000, about half of whom were dead. On the other hand, the Japanese home islands had two million men prepared to fight to the death in the event of invasion and intent on exacting the maximum loss to the invaders. In the Pacific island fighting, few Japanese combat troops surrendered. The capture of an island meant the annihilation of virtually all the defenders. In the Pacific the estimated battle dead for Japan was 965,000 men. American dead as a rule amounted to about ten per cent of the Japanese forces facing the attackers.

Death and wounding by conventional weapons are as real as those from nuclear bombs. Continuation of the conventional war without the use of the atomic bombs not only most probably would have meant one or two million additional dead for Japan's young fighting men, but also the death of several hundred thousand American combat troops and many hundreds of thousands of Japanese civilians.

In addition, perhaps millions of Japanese would have been wounded and other millions starved to death before the military opposition would have been completely crushed. Even as it was, the conventional bombing preceding the nuclear bombs had killed more people than the two atomic bombs.

Viewed in this light, the decision by President Truman to drop the atomic bombs saved the Japanese from a havoc from which it is not likely that they would have recovered for many decades to come. Moreover, no theoretical exposition of the terrible effects of nuclear war could have been brought home to the world's peoples in the way that this small sample demonstrated, and this is an additional if grim side benefit of Hiroshima and Nagasaki. Despite the terrible effects of atomic destruction, the use of the atomic bombs prevented far more potential suffering than occurred at Hiroshima and Nagasaki. Their use to end the Pacific War should not be regretted on either side, except as all warfare should be looked upon as a calamity to mankind.

VII *Our Strategic Base Organization*

THE Allied victory over Japan brought a great shrinkage of Japanese control over Pacific territory. Although the American Naval and Air Forces were actually responsible for Japan's defeat in the North Pacific as well as in the Central Pacific, the Soviet Union seized the Kurile Island chain as its prize for having joined the war against Japan, when it was already virtually won, ten days before Japan's surrender. Russian territorial control thus was brought to within about 20 miles of Hokkaido in Kunashiro Island, southernmost island of the Kuriles.

In the disposition of the southern part of Japan's former island empire the United States had clear rights to deciding what should be done. The price that the United States had paid for the former mandated islands of Micronesia in blood, labor and treasure was too high and the islands too valuable strategically to be relinquished by the United States in the foreseeable future. This right was confirmed by the United Nations not only in their agreement to making the United States the trustee power controlling the former Japanese Mandates, but also in their recognition that the United States had the right (not accorded to Japan in the League Mandates) to fortify and exclude from second nation access those islands that the United States considered strategically important to their security.

Moreover, by the terms of the United States peace treaty with Japan, the latter agreed that the Bonin and Ryukyu islands should remain under American control until such a time as tension in East Asia will have subsided and ceased to be a threat to international peace. It is on this basis that the United States has built up its highly important advance base on Okinawa in the center of the Ryukyu chain.

The liberation of Taiwan from Japanese control also was largely won by American forces, and no direct contribution to this was made by Chinese forces, Nationalist or Communist. The United States recognizes ultimate Chinese sovereignty over Taiwan as it does Japan's ultimate sovereignty over the Ryukyus, and for this reason it gave over its administration to the then legal and de facto Government of China. Nevertheless, this does not erase the rightful interests of the United States in what happens to the people of this strategic island for whom the United States won freedom from Japanese exploitation and domination. However, the United States exercises neither base rights nor control in Taiwan, and has aid personnel on the island only at the request and consent of the Chinese government to which the island was delivered at the end of the war.

STRATEGIC CHANGES

The result of the Pacific War brought a great change in the strategic and political organization of the Pacific Islands. Japan has become a friend and ally, and the potential threat to United States security has switched to the Soviet Union. The Soviet Union now controls the gateways into the Sea of Okotsk and the approaches to the Far Eastern and East Siberian coasts. Petropavlovsk on Soviet Kamchatka is no longer neutralized by the presence of a hostile Japanese naval and air base at nearby Paramushiro. The Soviet Union also is in a much superior position to bring pressure to bear upon Japan in order to obtain concessions and to ensure that Japan avoids policies inimical to Soviet interests. Aside from the military aspects of this superior position, it now controls former Japanese fishing grounds off Sakhalin and the Kuriles still much needed by Japan to sustain its people and its export trade.

For the United States, the forward line of strategic defense has advanced beyond the former untenable position running from Attu to Midway, Wake, Guam, and Manila Bay. Okinawa now is a front-line base of immense strategic importance 1229 miles in advance of Guam and bordering on the East China Sea. Here it is within easy support distance of the United States allies in Korea, Japan, Taiwan and the Philippines. A radius of 850 miles includes the hearts of all these lands. It is only about 500 miles to the eastern China coast. Okinawa as a base has certain weaknesses, and its strength depends partly upon the attitude of the four allies mentioned. Their friendly support provides secondary strategic facilities that protect Okinawa's flanks and extends its striking power. Also important is the attitude of the half-million Okinawans from whom land has been bought or leased for base facilities and who supply both fresh produce and labor power to fill the needs of the base and its personnel. Okinawa is mainly important strategically as an airbase. Its position is too exposed and too near potential enemies to permit the establishment of a major fleet base. Okinawa also suffers the disadvantage of lying squarely athwart the west Pacific typhoon paths.

THE BASES AT GUAM AND OAHU

More important in some ways than the extension of the United States base system to Okinawa has been the removal of threats to previously existing bases at Guam and Oahu. Guam's vulnerability to the Japanese attacks from Saipan and Tinian, Truk and the Marshalls during the start of the Pacific War needs no review here. With the removal of hostile control over the Marianas, Carolines and Marshalls there no longer are flanking threats posed to Tutuila or Guam, nor can these be used as advanced bases to support unexpected thrusts at Hawaii.

Guam is important as a main fleet base, as a major air base, and as Headquarters of the Pacific Strategic Air Command. It is the only land area between Pearl Harbor and the Philippines of sufficient size and having sufficient fresh water to construct the necessary shore-based facilities to support a main fleet base. Protected waters for large naval ships and submarines are available, while adjacent Saipan can accommodate destroyers and smaller craft. For the most part, these islands lie outside the usual paths of tropical typhoons. Guam, moreover, is American territory with no question concerning its future disposition, as in the case of Okinawa. From a naval point of view, the holding of Guam secures the line of communications from the United States to Australia and New Zealand. Its line of communications to Pearl Harbor is 3318 miles, while in the west it is 1340 miles to Iloilo in the Philippines.

Pearl Harbor is the heart of the United States Pacific defense system. From here the Commander-in-Chief of the Pacific Fleet directs all operations in the Pacific. The headquarters of other military services in the Pacific are likewise situated on Oahu. Reserves of man power and materials are available here and sent to the bases on Guam, Okinawa, Japan and the Philippines. Repair facilities for ships, planes and equipment are situated on Oahu. It is a nerve-center for the United States communications net in the Pacific, and large, comfortable hospitals and recreation and rest centers have been provided for the use of the armed forces. On the other hand, protected waters are available for only a limited number of ships, although anchorage in open roadsteads is available in the Hawaiian group for the major part of the United States fleet. A marine base at Kaneohe Naval Air Station on the windward side of Oahu was developed after 1951 to supplement Hickam Field and other fields on Oahu. Airfields also are available on the other major islands of the group.

THE IMPORTANCE OF THE PHILLIPINES

Collectively perhaps even more important than Okinawa in the front-line base organization are the Philippines facilities granted to the United States through treaty arrangements. Such areas as Clark Air Force Base and the installations at Iloilo are available not only for the security of the Philippine nation but also for the security of the sea lanes to the Indian Ocean from the Pacific and as flank protection for Guam and the Carolines Trust Territory. Iloilo has protected anchorages for the entire fleet if needed, with convenient exits to north, east, south and west in the Philippines area. It is south of the main typhoon paths, and there are suitable contiguous areas for land and seaplane bases. Its situation surrounded by numerous protected landplane bases requires only limited ground defenses aside from anti-aircraft. It has the advantage of nearness to potential supplies of fuel oil and petroleum products in Indonesia, and to supplies of foodstuffs in Australia and New Zealand as well as in the Philippines itself. Climatic conditions are much more favorable than normal for an area of such low latitude, and there are large supplies of fresh water. Clark Air Force Base, as well as other air bases available to the United States, lies only about 500 miles from Hong Kong and the South China coast and even closer than this to Taiwan. Although not situated in United States-owned territory, the ninety-nine-year security treaty arrangements with the Philippine Republic provide long-term use of the facilities.

SECONDARY UNITED STATES BASES

Secondary and supporting bases for the forward main base installations include Chichijima in the Bonins, where the United States has a naval station and a port of call for submarines, and Iwo Jima, which has an excellent air strip and which is used as a refueling point for United States Air Force planes.

Midway, 1300 miles from Honolulu, and Wake, 2308 miles from Honolulu and 1185 miles from Midway, have naval airfields as intermediate bases guarding the approaches to Hawaii. The battle of Midway in World War II proved its usefulness. However, the air base at Kwajalein, together with the unlimited anchorages available in the lagoon of this largest atoll in the world is much more important. Small marine repair facilities also are available here. Kwajalein occupies an important role in the Military Air Transport system and is a major stopover for trans-Pacific air flights. In 1961 it became a strategic missile-launching site. Johnston Island, between Hawaii and Kwajalein, has a limited role as an emergency airfield for naval and Military Air Transport planes.

PEACE TIME BASE REDUCTION

With the South Pacific Islands in friendly hands, the United States military requirements at Tutuila have become negligible, and in fact, the United States Navy no longer maintains a base here, although Pago Pago has a magnificent land-locked harbor. In the event of another major war, Tutuila's strategic situation almost on the Great Circle route between the United States and New Zealand and Australia would give it renewed importance. In both the Marshalls and Carolines, former air and naval bases fortified by the Japanese during their period of control now no longer are regarded as of such strategic significance as to require their incorporation into the United States defense-base system during peace time. Thus such islands as Yap, the Palaus, Truk and Ponape in the Carolines, and Jaluit, Eniwetok, Wotje, Maloelap and Mille in the Marshalls have been abandoned by the armed forces, and many of the former airfields are overgrown with weeds and shrubs. On the other hand, should need for them ever arise for sheltering a fleet or supporting air communications, their functions could be restored.

THE ALEUTIAN BASES

Protecting the northern approaches to the American continent are the Aleutians, where numerous islands have suitable sites for air bases. Their strategic importance led to Japanese occupation of Attu and Kiska in June of 1942. This forced the United States to develop a campaign for their recapture in mid-1943. Attu was regained after a major battle ending May 30, and Kiska on August 15, after the Japanese had deserted the island. The United States then constructed huge airbases at Cold Bay near the tip of the Alaskan peninsula, at Dutch Harbor on Unalaska, and at Adak, Amchitka, Shemya and Attu islands. Smaller army and navy installations were constructed on many lesser islands, including Atka, Kiska, and Tanaga, and these were stationed and maintained during the rest of the Pacific War. From these bases the American Air Force bombed the Kuriles repeatedly during the war, forcing the Japanese to retain numerous planes in the Kuriles for defense purposes.

Attu and Amchitka airbases were closed in 1947 and Dutch Harbor was closed in 1949. Shemya, Adak, and Cold Bay were scheduled to be closed in July of 1950, but the outbreak of the Korean War brought their reactivation. Continuing tension in Eastern Asia has required the continued maintenance of the bases at the latter three islands. Shemya and Cold Bay also have been used by commercial planes as refueling stops on the Great Circle route to Tokyo from North America. In view of the numerous hostile Soviet air bases in northeastern Siberia, Kamchatka, and the Kuriles, and of the important Soviet naval bases at Petropavlovsk and Paramushiro, the continued future strategic role of the 1000 mile long Aleutian chain of islands on our northwest defense line is assured.

THE ROLE OF MICRONESIAN BASES

In evaluating the role of the central Pacific island chains in United States possession or seized from the enemy during World War II, it is obvious that without the advance bases provided by them, the United States fleet could not have operated without the necessity of having many more ships and planes than it actually had. The Navy is well aware that a base to supply or repair fleet units several thousand miles closer to an enemy during warfare greatly multiplies the power that can be maintained constantly against him and greatly reduces the problems of logistic support and repair. This principle applies equally to the Air Force.

On the negative side, mere possession of a base means little. To be effective, a base must have the necessary men, equipment, facilities, weapons, and ships or planes. Moreover, as a minimum the investment in men and money at any base can only be considered adequate when the force maintained at the base is greater than any which a potential enemy could reasonably be expected to send against it. The financial burden of maintaining distant bases thus must be taken into consideration in viewing the strategic role of Pacific islands during peacetime. It is for this reason that many islands with fine natural facilities once used for air or naval bases in the Pacific now have been abandoned. The wisdom of this complete abandonment is questionable, however. Some islands, such as Bikini and Eniwetok in the Marshalls, have been used for nuclear weapons testing areas because of their relative geographic isolation and downwind situation that minimizes fallout danger to other islands. This also is true of Christmas island in the Central Pacific, used by the British for similar purposes.

MOBILE BASES IN WARTIME

The character of the base functions served by some of the Marshalls and Caroline atolls during the Pacific War is worthy of note, as it gives an idea of their potential usefulness at some future time. In the fall of 1943 the United States Navy issued orders for the organization of two mobile floating bases, one to leap-frog over the other as the fleet advanced across the Pacific. Service Squadron Four, formed first, was based at Funafuti in the British Ellice Islands. However, the fleet actually never made this atoll a base, but rather continued to return central Pacific fleet units needing repair to Pearl Harbor and southern Pacific fleet units to Espiritu Santo in the New Hebrides. With the taking of Majuro and Kwajalein during the first phase of the Marshalls campaign, the Funafuti Service Squadron was ordered to Kwajalein to provide services for vessels using the lagoon for anchorage. At this time Service Squadron Ten had been organized and was sent to Majuro Atoll to service the Fifth Fleet based there. Thereafter, although individual vessels sometimes were sent to Pearl Harbor or the Continent for repair, the Fleet as a whole stayed in the forward area and was serviced by Squadron Ten.

In April 1944 the two service squadrons were combined. The Fifth Fleet remained at Majuro until June, when it moved to Eniwetok and was joined there by the amphibious force for the Marianas invasion. This meant an enormous increase in the service function. At Majuro only enough service facilities remained to take care of the patrol and escort vessels operating there. The support and bombardment groups and one of the groups of larger transports were assigned to Kwajalein, while other transport groups were sent to Eniwetok with the Fifth Fleet. Among the service ships were slow old tankers unsuitable for operational use but adequate for use in lagoon harbors or for floating-base movement between anchorages in the forward areas. The scope of the service function is indicated by the fact that there were some 300 vessels of different sizes in the Marianas invasion armada. One of the big problems involved was the supply of fresh water, since the atolls do not have such water in quantity. The larger ships distilled in excess of their own needs to supply the water tankers.

THE EXAMPLE OF ULITHI

While the Marianas campaign was still underway, preparations were made for the service demands in the invasion of the Palaus and Leyte. This involved a move to Ulithi atoll in the Western Carolines. A shore base was being prepared at Manus Island west of the Bismarcks, but this was not completed sufficiently to take care of the Third Fleet and the Seventh Fleet. The mobile floating base thus furnished the answer to the problem.

The decision to rely on the floating base meant a move of the mobile base facilities such as water and fuel tankers and repair ships, to Ulithi, a move which took two weeks and involved four separate group movements. Because many of the service ships had to be towed, the speed was rather slow, only about six knots. Protection had to be afforded against Japanese submarine attacks which later sank a new tanker at Ulithi and damaged another ship. Typhoon damage to barges and losses in boats also occurred. The problems of berthing in Ulithi was a major one, since vessels need ample swinging room, and there were present at one time, on February 7, 1945, a total of 492 vessels, excluding boats and barges. Nevertheless, during the Iwo Jima and Okinawa operations Ulithi became the hub of almost all naval operations in the Pacific.

THE NEED FOR SCATTERED BASES

The tremendous value of such protected coral reef enclosures as the deep water lagoons of Kwajalein, Eniwetok, and Ulithi in future strategic considerations is very clear, since they greatly reduce the problems of safe logistic supply bases in forward areas. On the other hand, the development of nuclear bombs of far-reaching power has made such large concentrations of ships in one lagoon or harbor extremely dangerous in the event of any future hostilities. The large number of potential lagoon anchorage areas among the atolls and almost-atolls of the Marshalls and Carolines lend themselves to a considerable measure of dispersion of facilities if they need to be used, and for this reason the complete abandonment of already developed facilities might seem penny-wise and pound-foolish.

VIII The Physical Character of the Pacific Islands

THE foregoing chapters have outlined the historical evolution of the ethnography and the political geography of the Pacific and have established the strategic role the islands have played in the past century of United States history. In view of the importance attached to the Pacific Islands under United States control, the physical and climatic character of the Pacific environments merits our next examination.

GEOLOGIC DIVISIONS OF THE PACIFIC

The Pacific basin is the largest body of water in the world and one of the earth's oldest features. In its upthrust fringes to the north, west and east are about three-quarters of the world's active volcanoes in a border of tectonic instability. The basin itself divides into two major regions.

The line of division between the two regions, sometimes referred to as the *andesitic line*, runs along the south fringes of the Aleutians westward to the eastern shores of Kamchatka, thence southward to the east of the Kurile, the Japanese, the Bonin, and the Mariana chains, and of Yap and the Palaus. From the Palaus the line runs eastward, skirting the northern fronts of Melanesia to as far as the eastern fringes of the Fiji Islands. It then turns southward to run past eastern New Zealand. In the larger eastern region there is a relatively stable tectonic foundation in which active volcanism is found only in the Hawaiian and Galapagos Islands. Furthermore, the volcanic rocks of the eastern region that have emerged into islands are all basaltic by contrast to the acid andesitic rocks in the western volcanic region. The western region contains numerous active volcanoes and recent eruptive rocks and lavas.

Adjoining and to the oceanward of such island chains as the Aleutians, Kuriles, Japanese, Bonins, and Marianas are some of the deepest trenches of the Pacific. These deeps also are found east of the Ryukyus and the Philippines, and of the Fiji and Tonga groups. The deeps may have developed in the downwarping of the sea floor from the immense weight of volcanic rock piled up in the adjoining island chains.

Westward of the andesite line there has been much folding and faulting, and metamorphism has produced gneisses, schists, slates and granites. Sedimentary rocks, clays, sandstones and carboniferous materials are widespread. Mineral ores are relatively abundant west of the line, whereas east of the line the basalts include few workable ores except for bauxite in the Hawaiian Islands.

THE NUMBER AND TYPES OF ISLANDS

In the enormous extent of the Pacific area only a small fraction of the surface is occupied by islands. Though unimpressive in total area, the islands are impressive in number, since there are many thousands of them. They range in size from small rocks a few hundred feet or less in diameter to such enormous islands as New Guinea, Borneo, Honshu, and North and South Islands of New Zealand, which are on the order of the size of all New England combined or of such a state as Oregon. Because of their variety, no classification system that has been devised is completely satisfactory for their enumeration. One such enumeration placed the number of "main islands" in the Pacific at 2650. However, a group such as the Philippines alone contains some 7000 islands of various sizes, so that what constitutes a "main island" is difficult to define. The largest island in some of the atoll groups may be so small as to be excluded from the count of "main islands," yet to leave the whole atoll out of the enumeration is unrealistic.

In general one may recognize three major categories of islands in the Pacific: those of volcanic origin; those of biohermic limestone (coral and coralline) origin, mostly atolls; and those of volcanic origin surrounded by coral reefs. The latter two categories are found only in tropical waters. Most volcanic islands in the tropical Pacific east of the Philippines and Indonesia have fringing or barrier reefs of coral and coralline limestone, but there are exceptions. In the eastern Pacific, westward drift of upwelling cold water inhibits coral reef development, so that the Galapagos islands are not surrounded by such reefs. This factor also may be influential in inhibiting the development of reefs around the Marquesas Islands, although they lie only 300 miles north of the Tuamotu atolls and nearer the equator. The coast off the river mouths of some of the larger tropical islands such as New Guinea also may not have coral reefs, because corals are intolerant of fresh water and of the great amount of silt carried in suspension and deposited by rivers.

Within the area of American control in the Pacific, the only islands without fringing or barrier reefs are the Aleutians in the cool waters of the high latitudes.

THE VOLCANIC ISLANDS

The highest altitudes to which the volcanic mountains of the Pacific islands rise are found in New Guinea, where great ranges reach over 15,000 to as much as 16,500 feet. Eastward of New Guinea none of the volcanic islands reaches 10,000 feet, although in the Bismarcks and Solomons the highest elevations reach over 7000 and 8000 feet respectively above sea level. Still farther east the Fijis rise only to 4341 feet. In West Samoa one peak reaches 6094 feet and in Tahiti the maximum height rises to 7321. In the Marquesas the higher peaks are just a little over 4000 feet. On the other hand, in New Zealand Mt. Cook reaches 12,349 feet above sea level.

North of the Equator the highest elevation is found on the island of Hawaii where Mauna Loa is 13,680 feet high. Much smaller Oahu Island, however, rises only to 4025 feet. None of the Micronesian islands rise more than two or three thousand feet. Ponape is only 2595 feet high, and Yap and the Palau group are less than 800 feet high. The Marianas reach only 3166 feet, their maximum elevation on Agrihan Island. Guam and Saipan are 1334 and 1554 feet respectively in their highest peaks.

Whereas heights of almost 10,000 feet are found in the Philippines, and there are peaks over 10,000 feet high in Indonesia and in eastern Taiwan (highest 12,959), the Ryukyus are under 2,300 feet. Okinawa's highest point reaches 1650 feet. The Bonins are on the same order of elevations, Iwo Jima reaching 546 feet and Minami (South) Iwo reaching 3180 feet.

In Japan as in New Zealand, volcanism is very active and both areas have 10,000 feet high ranges. Mt. Fuji's 12,389 foot elevation in Japan is very comparable to the height of Mt. Cook in New Zealand. The islands of the Kurile chain drop down to levels of about 6000 feet at the most. Paramushiro at the northern end is 5955 feet high, while Kunashiro in the southern end reaches 6047 feet. In the Aleutians, the western islands are lower than the eastern ones, and the order of heights is shown by comparing the 3050 foot elevation of Attu at the west end with the 9878 foot elevation of Unimak at the eastern end of the chain.

It is clear, of course, that higher elevations require broader bases to support them, so that most of the higher elevations are found on the larger islands, although this correlation cannot be carried too far. The great weight of high volcanic masses that presses down upon the thin earth's crust at the bottom of the deep oceans reaches a maximum where towering ranges adjoin oceanic deeps, as they do on the east coast of Japan and on the east coast of New Zealand. Here differences between the deeps and the mountain tops may reach over 45,000 feet, or over eight miles. Such enormous pressure results in faulting and landslips that give rise to earthquakes, which in turn may lead to the development of tsunamis or "tidal waves". At Hawaii, Mauna Kea and Mauna Loa rise from a sea bottom over 18,000 feet deep to over 13,000 feet above sea level. The weight of the volcanic mass is such that the underlying crust is depressed. In compensation for the moat-like depression around the base of the island, there is an anticline rise bordering the outside of the depressed ring. However, earthquakes are not significant phenomena in the Hawaiian Islands.

The volcanic mountains of significant height above sea level possess certain attributes not found on coral atolls and reef islands. Elevation brings changes in temperatures. Sufficient changes in temperature result in the development of zonal changes in flora and fauna, ameliorate the hot humid conditions of low tropical areas, or lead to uncomfortable extremes in the high latitude regions such as in the Aleutians, in New Zealand's South Island, or in Japan's Hokkaido. Even New Guinea, which lies near the Equator, has boreal conditions and glaciers in the highest parts of its mountains.

A second attribute of the higher volcanic mountains is the obstacle they present to moisture bearing surface winds. Forced to higher elevations in order to cross the obstacle, the moisture in the winds condenses to precipitate in rain or snow on the windward slopes and in the peak areas. The peaks of mountains higher than 1000-2000 feet in the trade-wind zone are shrouded in clouds during a large percentage of the time and vegetation drips with moisture. Having become less moist in crossing the mountain, these winds then move downslope, warming up with lower altitudes and expanding their capacity to hold moisture. Instead of precipitating rain on the leeward slopes, the downslope wind may even increase the evapo-transpiration on such slopes. The leeward slopes thus lie in the rain-shadow of the mountain. Where, as in the trade-wind belt, prevailing winds normally come from one major direction, there may be very considerable differences in the average annual precipitation of the windward and leeward sides of a mountain. The windward side may be extremely wet and well vegetated while the leeward side may be arid and have desert-type vegetation. Even on the windward slope rainfall increases radically upslope.

The orientation of a mountain range as well as its elevation is important in the precipitation over the island as a whole. If the island is aligned with the wind, so that the wind merely bifurcates to flow parallel to both slopes of a mountain, very little rainfall may result in the lower slopes where no orographic lifting of air masses occurs.

A third attribute of volcanic mountains differing from the coral atolls or uplifted reef limestone islands is the water holding capacity of the ground. The fractured character of volcanic rocks often results in the capture of much of the rainfall in cracks that might otherwise result in surface run-off. If an impervious layer underlies and surrounds the lower part of the fractured rock, a considerable reservoir of water can be held and can be tapped by tunnels. On the other hand, fringing reefs of volcanic islands that become capped by lava flows may have fresh water held in the surface layers by impervious lava above the porous reef limestone. This fresh water can be tapped by wells, but if the wells are drilled so deeply as to penetrate the impervious layer, saline water may be reached and drawn into the pumps.

Volcanic islands of sufficient size also provide more shelter from violent storms for vessels in leeward waters. Coral atolls and reef islands provide only partial protection from winds, since they seldom rise more than 20-30 feet above sea level.

THE CORAL ATOLLS AND REEF ISLANDS

Although not as numerous as volcanic islands, coral atolls still number in the hundreds and reef islands in the thousands. Except for minute percentages of other minerals, limestone forms virtually the sole constituent of atoll rock. For the most part atolls comprise coral and coralline reef limestone caps over volcanic mountains, although some evolve on continental shelves.

The familiar Darwinian theory of atoll evolution generally accepted today holds that atolls develop from reefs that grow in the shallow water fringing a volcanic island located in water whose temperature does not fall for extended periods below 68°F. The reefs may be largely of coral structure or of coralline algae or, more commonly, of a combination of both. Holes and crevices in the reefs become partly filled and cemented with gravels, silts and sediments derived from both coral and coralline algae as well as from skeletal debris from other organisms and from calcareous precipitates from sea-water. Each generation of organisms builds upon the skeletons of previous organisms or on the conglomerated reef rock. Because sunlight is essential in the life-processes of reef-builders, reefs do not form at great depth into which light penetrates little or not at all. Usually reefs grow poorly and extremely slowly in depths below about 250 feet, and they flourish best in depths shallower than about half this. The width of a reef fringing a volcanic island in part depends upon the sharpness of slope of the foundation. Shallow water extending far from land thus would result in wider fringing reefs.

When a wide reef fringes a volcanic island, the near-shore sectors of the reef tend to be less flourishing than the seaward fringes for several reasons. The agitation of the water at the surge zone provides aeration and chemical conditions in the sea water more conducive to reef growth. Possibly more abundant plankton are brought over the reef by new innundations of sea water in the outer zone. Near shore the fresh water drainage from the volcanic island and the suspended sediments as well as the silt carried along by streams to the coast all create conditions that bring death or retarded growth to reef building corals. Thus the outside zones of a fringing reef flourish while the inner zones tend toward decay.

If in the course of time the great weight of the volcanic mountain causes it to sink or if there is a downward warping of the underlying crust and no new outpourings of lava build up the island, the volcanic land will gradually become submerged. The fringing reef, however, continues its growth upward and, in the case of existing atolls, the rate of reef growth has proved as fast or faster than the rate of sinking of the volcanic foundations. In its inner fringes the less favorable conditions for reef growth result in a widening of the gap between shore and the encircling reef, causing the development of a lagoon. At first shallow and narrow, this lagoon becomes deeper and wider with further sinking of the island. Gaps in the encircling reef, now called a barrier reef, may result from the inhibiting of reef growth by earlier fresh-water river mouths or from some other poor reef condition such a storm destruction. These become passes from the open sea into the lagoon. In this stage the island as a whole is sometimes called an almost-atoll. Truk is an example of this half-stage in atoll development. In time further sinking will result in the complete submergence of all the volcanic rock inside the barrier reef, leaving only the barrier reef at tide level or above. This final stage is a complete atoll, an oval or irregular ribbon of reef around an expanse of relatively shallow water.

In the beginning stages of formation the lagoon is a narrow ring of water around the volcanic island. In this stage the entire drainage of fresh water from the reef enclosure drains into the narrow lagoon, so that the lagoon is well diluted with fresh water, especially during heavy rains. However when the volcanic island remnants have almost disappeared or have sunk entirely, the rainfall received not only is much diminished because of the disappearance of the orographical lifting mechanisms, but what is received is now mixed with a larger volume of salt water held in a larger and deeper lagoon. Conditions thus once again become favorable for reef growth in the lagoon area. In most atolls there are many patches of reef, some of which have reached the surface and grow laterally as well as upward. Some reef patches cover areas half a mile across in the lagoon. Others are only a few yards across. Below the surface a lagoon may have hundreds or thousands of coral knolls or pinnacles in varying stages of growth toward the surface. On some atolls the lagoons either are not accessible to ships or boats owing to a lack of sufficiently deep channels through the reef, or there may be so many patch reefs and near-surface coral knolls that a vessel would find it extremely dangerous to navigate in such a lagoon.

In some atolls lagoons may be very shallow, in others rather deep. The majority of the larger lagoons reach depths of about 150 feet. Lagoons over 250 feet deep are rare. Smaller atoll lagoons may be only 50-70 feet deep. All lagoons are relatively shallow compared with the 10,000-15,000 feet oceanic depths from which the atolls rise. Reef building and lagoon sedimentation in time form limestone caps that deep drills have found to be up to 4000 feet thick.

ATOLL ISLAND CHARACTERISTICS

Atolls that are completely submerged at high tide hardly merit the name of island. However on most atoll reefs are piles of rubble constructed by storms or remnants of emerged reef that rise enough above high tide to form islands. Where these are large enough to accumulate a fresh-water film or "lens," pioneer plants from drift seeds or from seeds deposited by birds or winds become established. Soon a vegetated island appears. Currents in the lagoon frequently move sand and deposit it on the lagoon shore of already established islets on a reef and thus build up the islet area lagoonward.

Along most reefs the islets that form are not continuous land strips but usually comprise a number of islets of varying sizes. These are separated by shallow channels which may be from only a few inches to a foot or two in depth at low tide, though at high tide waist-deep streams of sea-water may rush across these channels, interrupting communications by foot between islets. The islets are usually at their widest at outward bends of the reef, because here lagoon currents and waves from the two outer sides of the reef-bend push sediments to fill in the corner of the lagoon. In such situations islets may reach 400-500 yards or more in width. Along other stretches of reef the islets may be very long, sometimes more than ten miles, but they usually are not more than one or two hundred yards wide. Typhoons striking such reef areas may push ocean water with erosive force across the rubble islets and wash out large parts down to the level of the reef flat, or they may cut channels to divide one islet into several smaller ones. Atoll land thus may be relatively impermanent. An atoll reef may have only two or three islets or as many as 100-200. The average number is 10-20.

An inhabitant of an atoll is well aware of certain peculiarities of reef islets that are not always obvious to the casual visitor. The latter can easily recognize by walking about several reef islets that most of the land rises only from a few feet to a maximum of about

10-15 feet above normal high-tide line. A visitor also will notice that near the seaward beach there is likely to be a ridge rising back of the shore, resulting from storm waves. These ridges usually are the highest parts of the land and consist of boulders, cobbles and pebbles. If the visitor is observant he will find that the seaward half of the islet usually is of much coarser debris and sediments than the material making up the lagoon half of the islet, where sand and finer pebbles commonly occur. There also may be beach ridges on the lagoon sides of an islet. The greater porosity of the seaward half often allows saline water to infiltrate into the subsurface "soil" and bring about unfavorable ground-water conditions for many atoll plants. In the lagoonward half the finer materials form a less permeable ground where fresh water generally may be found. Shallow wells often are dug 50-100 feet from the lagoon beach to tap this water.

However, the reef rock as a whole is usually so porous that water drains readily through until underlying salt-water is reached. Since fresh water has a lower density than salt water, in places where the presence of fine sediments prevents ready intermixture of fresh and salt water through circulation, rainwater draining downward floats on the salt water underneath. If an atoll gets sufficient rainfall a considerable depth of fresh water accumulates, and its weight presses down on the underlying salt water in the reef rock. The layer of fresh water builds up a "head" which drains off toward the periphery of the islet and out onto the beach and lagoon.

The central lagoonward part of the islet thus holds the deepest layer of fresh water, and the body of fresh water forms a "lens," thick in the middle and thinning towards the islet fringes. The difference in fresh and salt water density is such that fresh water in the center of the "lens" rising an inch above sea-level will have a thickness of 40 inches below sea-level, and a foot of fresh water above sea-level means 40 feet of "fresh" water beneath.

This principle is true in the abstract, but in actuality the lower portion of the fresh-water "lens" on an island is brackish for the thickness corresponding to the difference between high and low

ATOLLS of the PACIFIC

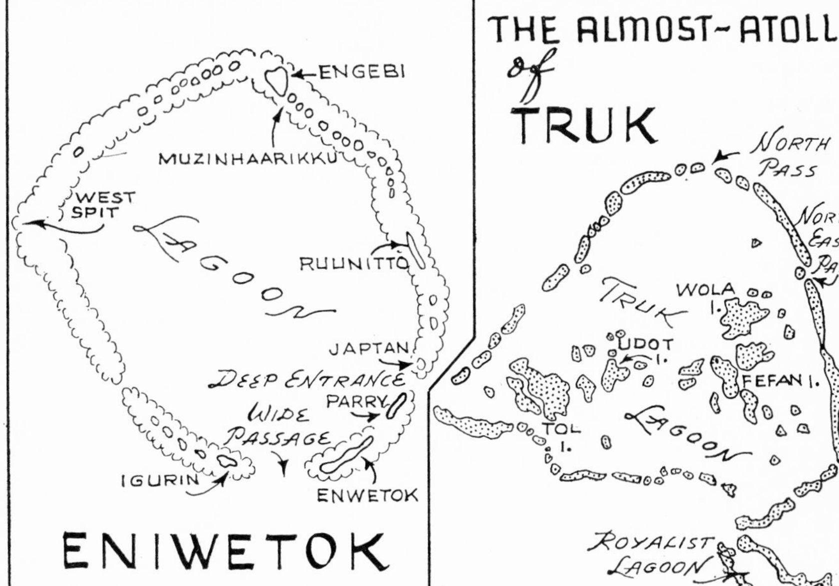

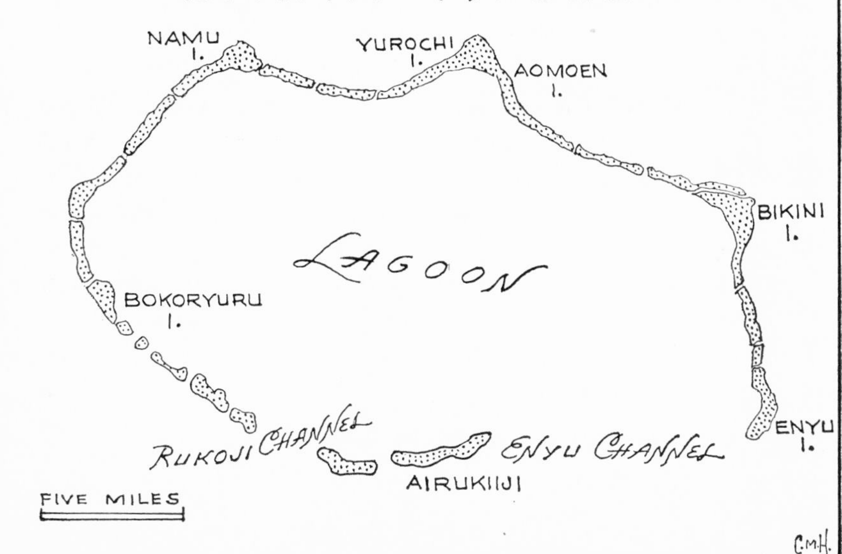

tide. This is so because the porosity of the reef rock permits the pressures of the tidal rises and falls to be exerted through the interstices of the islet rock materials. Water in a well dug in the middle of a reef islet rises and falls with the tide, although with a lag and not necessarily with the same amount of rise and fall as the tide. At low tide the withdrawal of tidal pressure brings a drop of fresh water in the "lens." But films of salt water are left behind around the earth or rock particles. The lower part of the fresh-water "lens" sinking into this salt-impregnated layer becomes brackish. Thus only the water in the "lens" above this zone is fresh.

Because of the differences in the thickness of the fresh-water "lens" there often is a zonation of vegetation on larger reef islets from the beach inward toward the center. This is especially observable on the islets where man has planted salt-sensitive food plants and trees such as taro, breadfruit, banana, lime and certain ornamental plants. Those plants that are intolerant of brackish water or of salt spray grow best in the heart of the islet where the fresh-water "lens" is thickest.

One may sum up the unique characteristics of atoll land as contrasted with volcanic islands in the following terms: extremely low altitudes of all land surfaces; underlying rock almost entirely porous limestone, with fluctuating fresh-water "lenses" where islets are large enough and rainfall high enough; usually narrow fragmented land areas separated by shallow reefs; and communications between distant parts of the reef usually must be done by boats or canoes. The only economic minerals on atolls or reef islands is phosphate, which occurs in exploitable quantity and quality on very few atolls.

ALMOST-ATOLLS AND RAISED ISLANDS

Almost all atolls essentially are atolls whose foundations have not subsided enough to submerge the enclosed volcanic peaks rising from their lagoons. Their lagoons usually are relatively shallow compared with those of ordinary atolls. The volcanic islands within them also have fringing reefs. Vegetated and inhabited low coral islets may occur on the reef encircling the lagoon of an almost-atoll.

One islet type yet undescribed is the uplifted reef island, such as Ocean or Nauru. Islands of this type may have been atolls at one time or sea-level reefs which have been tectonically uplifted dozens or hundreds of feet. Their surfaces are not very high, so that they have little orographical effect upon precipitation or temperature conditions on the land. Often their soluble limestones may be eroded into irregular pinnacles and declevities, caverns and fissures. They have no permanent surface streams as a rule. They present an abrupt cliff front dropping down to a fringing reef which makes approach from the sea difficult and access to the upland surface a hard climb.

IX *Patterns of Pacific Oceanography and Climates*

IN CONSIDERING air pressure systems, the air and water circulations and the temperature patterns of the Pacific area, one finds dynamic zones of change rather than static compartmentalized patterns. And in trying to begin the descriptions of the various processes involved, one finds each so inter-related with the others that it is difficult to pick a logical starting point. Perhaps the best way to initiate the discussion is to begin with the motion of the earth in its revolution about its own axis, for this motion affects both the water circulation of the Pacific Ocean and the air-mass movements above it. Moreover, the tilting of the earth's axis with respect to the sun shifts the thermal zones northward and southward of the equator with the seasons. This brings corresponding effects upon the air masses. This earth tilt provides general limits for the tropics at 23½ degrees north and south of the Equator. Within this ocean realm occurs the greatest amount of heating, the expansion of air-masses and the development of updrafts. Toward this region centering along the thermal equator air masses converge from cooler, higher latitudes on both sides of the Equator.

THE CORIOLIS EFFECT

The Equatorial circumference is the largest among the latitudes, while other latitudes dwindle in circumference northward and southward. This brings about a differential in the inertial drag of water floating upon the earth's surface at different latitudes and of the air above it. The water and the air-masses at the Equator tend to drift westward in the opposite direction from the revolution of the earth. This motion is represented in the prevailing westward Equatorial currents as well as in the trade wind drift. In addition to this effect is that known as the *coriolis* effect produced by the earth's sphericity and its revolution around its axis. The expression of this effect lies in the tendency of air-mass movements and water circulations to be diverted to the right of the path of movement in the northern hemisphere and to the left of the path of movement in the southern hemisphere. This effect becomes less marked in the immediate vicinity of the geographic Equator and becomes zero at the Equator, since here the opposite effects in the two hemispheres are neutralized. Away from the Equator the effect strengthens.

THE OCEAN CURRENTS

Let us first examine the effects upon the ocean currents. In theory, at least, the westward drift of the water on both sides of the Equator should show a curve away from the Equator, and in fact toward the western side of the ocean the currents in the trade-wind zone do exactly this. Since land masses in the western Pacific block the continued westward drift, waters of the northern Equatorial current are diverted northward past the Philippines, the Ryukyus and southern Japan, bringing warm water averaging 80°-81° F. to higher latitudes in the northwest Pacific. Since the Pacific is almost landlocked in the north, much of this warm water continues eastward in a great whirl past the Aleutians to the coasts of Alaska and northwest North America, cooling gradually as it moves farther north. The contour of the northwest American coasts helps direct the waters of this so-called Kuroshio or Japan Current southward and then back southwestward to complete the great clockwise whirl around the Pacific. In the South Pacific the openness of the ocean around Antarctica leads to a less well defined counterclockwise whirl, although this also occurs.

However, upon this simple scheme of major oceanic circulation are superimposed many complexities. Divergence of water away from the Equatorial regions on both sides of the Equator requires upwelling of water in the Equatorial zone to take the place of the water that has moved away. Also, in the eastern side of the ocean in the Equatorial zone, the westward oceanic drift brings about upwelling from the depths near the continents to replace the surface water removed. This upwelled water is rather cold even though it rises to a subtropical and tropical surface region. The effect of this cold water joining the westward drift reaches far to the west and may even be influential in inhibiting coral reef growth around the French Marquesas Islands.

In the western side of the North Pacific not all of the currents of the westward drift are diverted toward the north into the Japan Current or into the South Pacific. Some of it penetrates the seas and basins of Indonesia and of the Philippines to form local circuits. There also is a major reversal of current direction around the Palau Islands, south of which an eastward flow starts between the two branches of the westward drift north and south of the Equator. This is called the Equatorial Counter Current, and it runs nearly all the way across the Pacific. Actually, however, the Counter Current always lies north of the Equator, and its position shifts seasonally from one near the Equator during the southern summer to a position one or two degrees farther north during the northern summer. The Counter Current during February-March flows past the southern side of the Caroline Islands in the west and runs between Ponape and Kusaie in the eastern Carolines. It continues eastward between the southern Marshalls and the northern Gilberts, passing the last islands in the Central Pacific between Palmyra and Christmas.

The speed of the westward Equatorial drift is less than one knot in the northern current and up to as much as four knots in the southern current. The Counter Current is weaker and averages only about one knot. Among the various island groups the simple movement breaks up into complex gyrals and cross currents. In the western part of the Pacific the intensity of flow of the Japan Current as well as the southeast-turning Counter Current in the vicinity of the Palau Islands varies with the seasonal monsoon winds of East Asia. In winter the winds blow diagonally from the northeast against the Japan Current and with the southeast drift past northern New Guinea. In summer the winds move in the opposite direction and help speed up the Japan Current as well as move it nearer to the China coast. Near the southern Ryukyu Islands this current is some 2000 feet deep and runs at a rate of about 1.5 knots. Off Japan it has summer temperatures above 80° F. and late winter temperatures of 68° F.

A minor part of this current penetrates into the Sea of Japan to run as far north as southern Hokkaido. After the main Japan Current (Kuroshio) moves past Tokyo Bay, the westerlies and the Coriolis effect drives it east and northeastward across the Pacific. Part of the current flowing due eastward soon turns south to form a clockwise whirl reaching as far eastward as about 160° E. The main northeastward current runs as far eastward as 150° W., or to the longitude of central Alaska, by which time most of this drift has turned south and then southwestward toward the Hawaiian Islands. Paralleling the Japan Current and to its north is the Aleutian Current with lower temperature probably derived from mixing between cold currents and having lower salinity because of high precipitation. This cooler current becomes a counterclockwise whirl in the Gulf of Alaska, and part of it enters the Bering Sea through the eastern passes. In the Bering Sea the current is counterclockwise. Cold water from this drift moves as the Oyashio, or boreal, current southward past Kamchatka and the Kuriles to Hokkaido and northern Honshu. This seldom gets above 65° F. and is near freezing for several months of the year.

The branch of the southwest-moving current in the northeast Pacific forms a gyral which usually has its center northeast of Hawaii. Its position shifts with the season. Sometimes the center moves near Hawaii. At other times it moves northeastward so far that the southwest sector of the current brings Equatorial water as far north as the Hawaiian Islands.

PACIFIC TEMPERATURE AND HUMIDITY CONDITIONS

The temperature conditions within which the United States administers Pacific islands range from equatorial through subtropical to sub-boreal. Most of these islands lie in the tropical realm in which temperatures are always high, with monthly temperatures averaging around 82° F. the year around. Day and night temperatures, however, vary from a low of about 74° F. in the early pre-dawn to over 95° F. in mid-afternoon. Humidity is always high, and it is highest in the low-temperature period and lowest in the high-temperature period. Sensible temperatures differ importantly between areas exposed to the prevailing trade-winds and areas sheltered from them. Vertical temperature zonation occurs on all significantly elevated islands, of course.

The Ryukyu Islands is the only American administered area that may be considered subtropical with hot summers and mild winters influenced considerably by the situation of the islands near the continent of Asia. Average temperatures during summer are below 72° F. and in winter below 65° F. The winters average at least 11° F. warmer than the mainland China coast at the same latitude, and frost and snow are unknown.

The Aleutians, on the other hand, are in high latitudes, but their position is no higher than that of the British Isles. The average annual range moderated by the marine surroundings is only about 20° F. but August, the warmest month, averages only about 50° F. From January to February the average is about 30° F. The high humidity makes for uncomfortably chilly sensible temperatures most of the year.

PACIFIC AIR PRESSURES AND AIR MASSES

The wind systems of the Pacific develop chiefly around six major pressure systems, two of which are the complementary Asiatic and Australian seasonally reversing continental systems. Two others are the seasonally shifting permanent northeast and southeast Pacific high pressure "cells." The final two are low pressure troughs.

One of the latter is the Equatorial low pressure trough lying between the two Pacific highs; the other is the seasonally contracting and expanding Aleutian low.

In general, the oceanic high in the northeast Pacific creates a system of clockwise winds or an anticyclone which in its southern and southeast quadrant moves as the northeasterly and easterly tradewinds in the eastern and central North Pacific. In the Southeast Pacific the high pressure develops a counterclockwise wind around it which moves as the southeast and easterly trades south of the Equator. The shifting of the positions relative to the seasonal cooling and heating of North and South America and of the thermal belts over the Pacific brings some changes in the orientation and strength of the trades.

Changes in the wind direction in the trade-wind zone also are caused by wave-like motions in the pressure system moving westward. These are associated with the formation of cyclonic gyrals that travel westward in the trade-wind belt and at times develop into destructive tropical hurricanes or typhoons.

Northwest of the North Pacific high is the east-west elongated Aleutian low pressure trough which has great magnitude during the northern winter and reaches from the Gulf of Alaska coast to the northern Kuriles. The central part of the trough lies south of and parallel to the Aleutian chain and the Alaska peninsula. In summer the trough becomes very restricted and its center shifts slightly northward. As a result of frequent frontal clashes, this is an unpleasant region of cyclonic storms, gales, low clouds, fog, and drizzling rain, and in winter, stinging snow storms.

In the western Pacific, the prevailing easterly trade wind system is interrupted both north and south of the Equator by monsoonal wind shifts. In summer, when Central Asia develops a strong low pressure region, the widespread convectional updrafts draw in air from the Pacific and Equatorial regions to its east and south. Since Australia has its winter at the time Asia has its summer, the Australian anticyclone causes winds to move outward from the continent northward toward the Equatorial regions. The strength of the

Asiatic low pressure may draw air masses from the Australian region across the Equator into Asia. During the northern winter, the strength of the Asiatic high pressure in Mongolia and Siberia and the simultaneous existence of low pressure during the Australian summer reverses the preceding situation. Winds from north of the Equator then cross into the southern hemisphere. These prevailing seasonal southeasterly and northwesterly monsoon winds are felt in the Ryukyu, Mariana and western Caroline Islands. The Asiatic monsoon winds also affect the Kuriles but with stronger east and west components than in the tropics.

PACIFIC STORMS AND STORM PATHS

The eastern tropical Pacific is relatively free of storms except very near the continental coasts of Central America and Mexico, because the cold upwelled oceanic waters create relatively stable lower atmospheric conditions. West of the Marquesas the weak westward-traveling low pressure "cells" enter warmer waters, and the winds circulating around them tend to speed up with higher evaporation rates and greater instability of the moisture-saturated surface air masses. Many of these cyclonic gyrals evolve into destructive storms. Both north and south of the Equator the frequency and intensity of such typhoons or hurricanes increase toward the western fringes of the Pacific.

Within five degrees of the geographic Equator the much diminished coriolis effect and the lack of frictional drag of opposing winds greatly reduce the number of cyclonic gyrals with violent winds, and this zone for the most part is free of typhoons. However, many weak cyclones that later develop into violent typhoons may originate in this zone, and occasionally some typhoons have been recorded crossing the Equator from the North Pacific into the Southwest Pacific.

It is a well-known phenomenon that both north and south of the Equator the traverses of the typhoons move gradually away from the Equator toward the north and south. This may be attributed in part to the Coriolis effect; another cause may result from the fact that the equatorward sectors of these cyclonic gyrals have winds which oppose the easterly trades, whereas the polarward sectors have winds blowing with the trades. Thus, the retardation on the equatorward sector and the speed-up on the poleward sectors naturally produce northward and southward shifting gyrals. Of course not all storm paths are this consistent. In rare instances the paths or traverses will even form loops.

Storm paths of tropical typhoons north and south of the Equator have differing characteristics that appear to demonstrate some relationship to the position of the continental masses in these oceans and possibly to the major current trends. Thus, in the southern Pacific violent typhoons form much farther east than in the northern Pacific. In the North Pacific few westward-moving cyclonic gyrals reach typhoon intensity before the longitude of the Marshalls, and most of them reach this intensity only west of the 155th Meridian East, a thousand miles west of the Marshalls. In the South Pacific typhoons are well known in the Tuamotus, about 2,500 miles east of the longitude of the Marshalls. The typhoon paths are especially numerous between the Tongas and New Caledonia, that is, from the longitudes of the Marshalls eastward 600-700 miles.

Moreover, the typhoons of the northern tropical Pacific funnel into a much more concentrated and narrow zone in the extreme western Pacific between the longitudes 120° and 130° East. By contrast, in the Southwest Pacific there does not appear to be any such channeling of typhoon paths, which here are more evenly scattered from the Cook Islands to New Caledonia, a spread of 40 degrees of longitude compared with the 10 degrees of the western North Pacific. These situations correspond remarkably with the tropical oceanic currents. That is, the concentration of typhoon paths in the tropical North Pacific follows the course of the Japan Current, which becomes a much more restricted current than the broad sheet movements toward the southwest in the western South Pacific. However, in the South Pacific the recurvature of the typhoon paths toward the southeast as they reach higher southern latitudes is not followed to as marked a degree as that of the paths of typhoons and the Japan Current in the northern hemisphere.

Another noteworthy correlation is that the more eastward development of typhoons in the South Pacific and their more westward development in the North Pacific correspond roughly with the respective regions north and south affected by the reciprocal Asiatic-Australian monsoon air-flow. The more easterly position of Australia in the South Pacific creates monsoonal air-mass movements much farther eastward in the South Pacific than the monsoonal winds occur in the North Pacific. The orientation of the monsoonal air flow between Asia and Australia is southeast to northwest. Zonal lines connecting the regions where the cyclonic storms reach typhoon intensities north and south of the Equator correspond with and overlap the region of monsoonal air mass movements.

In the western North Pacific the period of most frequent typhoon occurrence is during the northern summer and fall (July-November). In the western South Pacific they are most frequent also during the southern hemisphere's summer and fall (December to March). In these seasons in the respective hemispheres, the monsoonal air flow brings large volumes of well-saturated warm and unstable Equatorial air masses to higher latitudes in the West Pacific than occurs farther east. Such air masses provide just the conditions for energizing cyclonic disturbances already developed or for bringing weak ones to full force. Moreover, the prevailing direction of the monsoons, just as in the case of the direction of the trades, tends to accentuate the movement of the storm paths away from the Equator and to shift to the right of the path of movement.

Samoa in the South Pacific lies in or near the path of some typhoons in their early stages of formation, but most of the southwest Pacific cyclones reach typhoon intensity only in somewhat higher latitudes. In the North Pacific the Marshalls atolls experience occasional typhoons, whereas the central and western Carolines from about the longitude of Truk and the Marianas experience them rather frequently. There appear to be two main typhoon channels west of the Marshalls, each about 200 miles broad. One runs past the south side of Guam. The other has an axis running past the south sides of Woleai and Ulithi. Thereafter they merge into one broad channel that follows the Japan Current in a curve past Taiwan, up the Ryukyu Chain, over Okinawa and through southern Kyushu. From here the chief route of typhoons curves northeastward past Tokyo Bay. The destructive effects upon islands in their paths are great. They are especially serious on low coral reef islands over which storm waters may completely sweep, washing out the land itself.

As these cyclones gyral into cooler latitudes they slow down considerably, become larger and form the less destructive extra-tropical cyclonic storms which move eastward across the Pacific in the west-wind regions of the middle latitudes. As mid-latitude cyclonic storms, they bring changeable and stormy weather to the Aleutian Islands. When they reach the Aleutians, these extra-tropical cyclones originating as tropical typhoons are hardly distinguishable from the cyclonic storms of continental origin moving with the westerlies out of central or northern Asia.

TSUNAMI "TIDAL WAVES" IN THE PACIFIC

The instability of parts of the sea floor of the Pacific basin occasionaly gives rise to submarine earthquakes which generate low waves with lengths from crest to crest of as much as 100-600 miles. Whereas wind waves seldom exceed about 60 miles per hour, these earthquake-generated long waves, known by their Japanese name of *tsunami,* sometimes travel over 500 miles per hour. In the open ocean their two-or-three-foot height is hardly noticeable, although the rapidity of travel gives a ship meeting such a wave the sensation of hitting something massively solid. However, when the *tsunami* reaches shallow water the continuing push of the long wave traveling at the speed of a fast airplane may pile up a frighteningly destructive wall of water 50-100 feet high that sweeps everything before it across the beach and far into the land. The withdrawal of the wave sucks everything in its path back to the sea.

Moreover, a *tsunami* is not limited to a single wave, but comprises a train of waves separated by intervals of calm water. The successive waves may come from a quarter of an hour to an hour apart. The characteristics exhibited are an initial low swell of little more than ordinary proportions followed by a sudden retreat of the shore waters, leaving wide stretches of former shallow water-covered seabottom exposed. The succeeding wave is quite destructive, but later ones may be even higher. The height may build up to the eighth wave, after which they become smaller and gradually cease. Both east and west shores of the Pacific have experienced the awesome destruction of these sudden waves. Japan possibly has suffered the most in this respect because of the greater frequency of nearby earthquakes. But since these waves travel all the way across the ocean, most exposed shores with gradually shoaling shelves may suffer destruction. Thus, Aleutian, Peruvian or Kamchatka earthquakes may cause serious *tsunami* damage in Hawaii and Japan. On a long-term basis Hawaii may be visited by an average of one very destructive *tsunami* in 25 years. The lives lost in Japan from *tsunami* on occasion have numbered many thousands. Loss of life and of property has greatly decreased as the result of recent seismic techniques of forecasting impending *tsunami*. Regions likely to be affected now may be given enough warning to permit people to leave in time.

Low coral atolls seem to suffer less from *tsunami* damage than the coasts of high islands facing the oncoming wave. The apparent reason for this is that atolls do not have shallow submarine shelves upon which they build high waves. Innundations may occur, however, and the amount of such innundations would seem to be greater where the contour of the reef tends to funnel waves into a more restricted area.

TIDAL MOVEMENTS IN THE PACIFIC

During the attack on Tarawa in the Pacific War tidal conditions turned out to be a highly important element creating difficulties for landing-craft attempting to cross the reef. Tides must be considered, of course, in attempts to enter harbors or sail through channels and reef passes. The tidal conditions create currents in lagoons, passes and reef vicinities, affecting ship and boat movements and anchorages. In considering the political geography of the Pacific, therefore, tidal variations deserve some consideration.

The Pacific basin is a semi-enclosed basin and behaves somewhat like a pan of agitated water. In addition to the tidal pull of the moon and sun, there are effects resulting from the oscillation of tides between continental shores and the shores of large islands. There develop nodes and amphidromes in the tidal harmonics where the tidal rise approaches zero and away from which the tides gradually rise to reach a maximum height. In the northern tropical Pacific the lowest tides are found along an eastward curving phase-transition node or line not quite meridional, running past the eastern side of the Marianas southwestward through the Woleai and Lamotrek area in the central Carolines. Along this elongated region the mean spring tidal rises are between 1.5 and 2.5 feet. Eastward and westward of this line the tidal rise becomes greater. Thus, westward in the Yap area the rise is about 4 feet and in the Palaus about 6 feet. Eastward at Ponape it is about 3 feet, at Ujelang 4.5 feet, at Arno Atoll in the Marshalls and Tarawa in the Gilberts, 6 feet.

Two amphidromes, or points of low tide, are found to the eastward of the Marianas tidal node. One is situated near the center of the Solomons; another at a point in the open ocean about 200 miles east of Malden atoll. In the Solomons where it is close enough to an island to be measured, the tidal rise is only about 6 inches. Around the point in the open sea the tidal rise cannot be measured, but on the atolls from Palmyra to the Tuamotus the tidal rises are only between 1.5 and 2.4 feet. Eastward in the Marquesas the rises are between 3 and 3.5 feet, and at Canton in the west it is 4 feet. Southward from the Ellices and Gilberts, where the rises are around 6 feet, the tides decrease to about 4.6 feet in the Samoan Islands and to around 4 feet in the low islands southeast of the Fijis.

Another feature of Pacific tides is the differing number of tidal rises and falls in various parts of the Pacific. The number depends upon the length of the period of an oscillation. Where the period is about 12 hours there will be one high and one low tide every 12 hours, or two highs and two lows every 24 hours. Where the period is 24 hours there will be only one high and one low during this period. Of course there are intermediate periods, as in the situation of the Hawaiian Islands, where there is the phenomena of two high tides and two low tides, but one high is lower than the other high. Thus, there is a "high" high tide and a "low" high tide.

In the Marshalls east of Ujelang and Eniwetok and at Kusaie, the tides are semi-diurnal, that is, having two highs and two lows in 24 hours. At Namonuito in the central Carolines the tides are diurnal, and they are mainly diurnal eastward and westward from Truk to Satawal. At Ponaps and the atolls in its vicinity the tides are predominantly semi-diurnal, as they also are in the Marianas, western Carolines, Yap and Palaus. Semi-diurnal tides occur southeastward of the Marshalls as far as the Samoa, Fiji and Tonga groups, and they are also found in the Societies and Tuamotus. West of the Fijis the tides are predominantly semi-diurnal, but in the Solomons and Bismarcks they are diurnal or predominantly diurnal.

PRECIPITATION ON PACIFIC ISLANDS

Because the atmosphere over the tropical oceans is highly charged with moisture at all times, any marked drop in the temperature to which the air masses are subjected will precipitate the moisture. Where islands present high and wide surfaces fronting prevailing winds, the likelihood of rainfall is high on the windward sides. Where the winds generally come from one primary direction, as occurs in the trade-wind regions, one side of the island will tend to be very wet most of the year and the average annual rainfall will be high. On the leeward side, to the contrary, there is likely to be a moisture deficiency that is reflected clearly in the differences in vegetation. Thus, it becomes difficult to describe patterns of average annual amounts of rainfall among the high volcanic Pacific islands, since each island has wide ranges from 10-20 inches in parts of an island to several hundred inches for other higher parts. The size and orientation of an island also account for differences. For the high islands, therefore, it is better to avoid general comparisons, since they are relatively meaningless. High island climatic patterns thus become very much individualized and should be described as individual patterns.

The chief large areal differences may be briefly summarized. That is, the highest average annual rainfalls are those occurring in tropical regions where vertical temperature differences are greatest. One does not encounter in the Aleutians the high rainfall amounts that are found in the Hawaiian Islands, for instance. On the other hand, the volume of the air masses uplifted to bring about precipitation is increased by the strength of the wind carrying the moisture. In this respect, there is larger areal differentiation in regional potentials for precipitation, for some parts of the Pacific have greater average wind speeds than others. Thus, rainfall is likely to be greater in the western parts of the tropical Pacific where frequency of typhoon occurrences is greatest.

It is also true that in the zone between the converging north and south Pacific trades lies an area in which there occur large-scale rising air masses which may bring comparatively large volumes of rain regardless of orography. Yet this is a principle that must not be taken to indicate fixed zones which invariably get high rainfall. This is seen in the great fluctuations in annual rainfall amounts on the low atolls that lie in the tropical Pacific. Thus, Onotoa in the Gilberts in 1946 had 85 inches of rainfall but in 1950 had only 6.6 inches. Fanning in 1905 recorded 208 inches but in 1950 received only 28 inches. Both of these are not far from the Equator.

Although such great variations from year to year do exist, these are exceptions, and long-term averages do work out into noteworthy patterns of rainfall over the tropical Pacific whose peculiarities leave much to be explained. If one were to draw an imaginary line from Wake Island at about 20° N. latitude through the Marshalls, Gilberts and Ellices to the Tongas, at about 20° S. latitude, the average annual rainfall amounts in the northern end of the line would be found to be only about 24 inches. Through the Marshalls there is a steady increase to about 107 inches at Kwajalein,

120 inches at Majuro, and 157 or more inches at Jaluit. This would appear to mark the region of highest rainfall along the line. Further southward the rainfall in the northernmost Gilberts, Butaritari, is 121 inches; farther south, at Tarawa 64 inches and at Tabiteuea 41 inches. From here southward through the rest of the Gilberts the amounts again increase steadily through the Ellices to reach another high rainfall region around Funafuti, where 144 inches is the average annual amount. Still farther southward the annual amounts again decline, so that between the Fijis and the Tongas the low island rainfall averages about 79 inches.

Similarly, a line drawn from Palmyra through the Tuamotus shows steady decreases southward from Palmyra's 150 inches to 58 inches at Christmas Atoll and 28 inches at Malden. From here there is an increase to 40-50 inches in the Tuamotus.

The causes for such variations are related to the complexities of differing air mass qualities, wave-motions in the pressure systems and the development of cyclonic gyrals resulting in air mass clashes.

In the Ryukyu Islands rainfall amounts at different stations vary, depending upon their locations on the east or west coasts of the islands. Naha on the west coast of Okinawa gets an average of 77 inches annually. Nase on the north coast of Amami O Shima farther north gets about 125 inches. The monsoon influences of Asia are strongly felt in the Ryukyus. Winter winds from Manchuria and Siberia curve clockwise over Japan and reach the Ryukyus from the northeast, bringing frequent rains. Summer winds from the south and southeast bring even more rain, and May and June with 10 and 8 inches respectively have the most rain of the 12 months at Naha. At Nase, June has the most rain with 16 inches, followed in order by August, May and October, each with over 12 inches. Each month in both places has at least four inches on the average, however, so that rainfall is well distributed the year around.

In the Marianas and Bonins farther east the monsoon influences continue to be felt, with about 60 per cent of the rain coming during the three summer months. Although orographical factors make comparisons less reliable than in the case of the coral atolls, there apparently is a decrease in rainfall from north to south. Rainfall in the central Bonins averages in the 60-inch range as compared with the 70-90 inches in the southern Marianas and Guam. Further southward rainfall in the sea-level stations of the Yap and Palau regions ranges between 100 and 120 inches.

In the sub-boreal islands of the Aleutians the precipitation averages less than half that in the Marianas and Bonins, varying from 25 to 50 inches. However, the low evaporation counters the need for high rainfall. Furthermore, the precipitation comes in light falls spread over about 250 days of the year, with sunshine further limited by frequent fogs. At Attu, in the extreme west end of the chain, five or six days a week are rainy, and there are scarcely a dozen clear days during the year. It is evident from the above discussion that although oceanic winds are usually saturated with moisture, the pattern of Pacific precipitation is a complex one.

X The Population Squeeze

Up to this point our discussion has been concerned with ethnography, historical events, and environment. It is now desirable to link these to the present demography and living space in the Pacific. Excluding the larger Asiatic countries, New Zealand, and New Guinea, and the military forces on temporary assignments, there now live in the Pacific islands approximately 2.3 million people. In 1958 about 1,600,000 of these inhabitants were under United States administration. Of the latter, 855,000 were in the Ryukyus and 613,000 were in the State of Hawaii. This leaves only about 127,000 distributed among the 187 island units (an atoll being counted as one unit) stretching from the Aleutians in the north to Samoa in the south, Hawaii in the east to Okinawa in the West. The total land of United States administered Pacific islands (excluding islands near the continental coasts such as the Catalina Islands or those of southern Alaska) amounts to an estimated 15,111 square miles. More than 13,000 square miles of this is divided nearly equally between the Aleutian and the Hawaiian islands, although the latter have about 120 times as many inhabitants as the former. The remaining island groups and islands share only 1,883 square miles of area, which is less than half that of the Bahamas in the Caribbean but which has almost twice as many people as the Bahamas.

MAN-LAND RATIOS ON PACIFIC ISLANDS

In analysing the relationships between the population and the land, it is helpful to refer to the following Table I listing the island groups and some of the chief islands. In the first part of the list are those islands under United States administration. In the second part

Table I (Part 1)

Demographic Statistics for Pacific Islands under United States Administration

Name	Area (sq mi)	Population	Date	Average Density of Population	Average Annual Population Increase (%)
Aleutian	6,821	5,521 (fewer than 700 Aleuts)	1950	0.8	
Hawaii	6,407	613,000	1958	96.0	
Guam	206	59,498	1950	280.0	
		65,000	1957	316.0	9.2
Mariana group	183.61	4,750	1948	25.8	
		8,220	1958	45.0	7.3
Yap	38.5	2,744	1948	71	
		3,176	1958	82.5	1.57
Palau group	188	5,900	1948	31	
		8,845	1958	47	5.0
Truk	38.56	9,510	1948	24.6	
		13,825	1958	36.0	4.3
Ponape	129	5,735	1948	44.4	
		9,843	1958	76.3	3.7
Kusaie	42.31	1,652	1948	39.2	
		2,510	1958	59.3	5.7
Marshall group	69.84	10,160	1948	145.0	
		13,728	1958	196.0	3.56
Caroline group	461.44	35,994	1948	78.0	
		48,446	1958	105.0	3.46
Caroline atolls total	24.59	9,496	1948	387.0	
		8,137	1958	331.0	1.67
U.S. Trust Territory (as a whole)	687	55,730	1948	81.0	
		70,724	1958	103.0	3.89
Ryukyu group (as a whole)	1,291	574,579	1940	443.0	
		1,012,764	1956	782.0	4.85
U.S. Administered portion of the Ryukyus	848	807,400	1956	744.0	
		855,000	1959	1,012.0	1.8
Daito Islands	18	2,691	1950	150.0	—
Bonin group	40	4,300 (130 natives)	1939	108.0	
		190	1958	5.0	
Volcano (Iwo) Islands	11	—			
American Samoa	73	18,937	1950	260.0	
		20,850	1957	286.0	1.4

Table I (Part 2)

Demographic Statistics for Pacific Islands Administered by Other States

Name	Area (sq mi)	Population	Date	Average Density of Population	Average Annual Population Increase (%)
Western Samoa	1,130	74,663	1950	65.5	
		97,327	1956	87.5	5.0
Gilbert and	369 (?)*	36,000	1948	96.0 (?)	
Ellice group		39,100	1956	107.0 (?)	1.09 (?)
Tonga group	269	44,448	1948	164.0	
		56,838	1956	210.0	3.43
Fiji	7,036	293,764	1950	42.0	
		345,737	1956	49.4	2.96
Solomon Islands Protectorate (excluding Bougainville	14,600	95,000	1947	6.5	
and Buka)		112,000	1958	7.7	1.65
New Hebrides	5,700	51,831	1948	9.1	
Condominion		53,959	1955	9.3	0.58
New Caledonia	9,401	50,000	1949	5.3	
		69,834	1956	7.4	5.77
French Oceania	1,544	60,000	1950	38.8	
		73,201	1956	47.4	3.68
Tuamotu atolls	330 (75)*	6,143	1946	18.5 (82.0)	
		6,615	1956	20.2 (88.6)	0.77

* The official figures for the Gilbert, Ellice and Tuamotu atolls appear too high to be accepted for the "land" areas of the atolls and probably include reef areas as well.

are other prominent island groups of the Central or South Pacific administered by other powers.

UNRELIABILITY OF STATISTICS

The table gives figures from a variety of sources, but largely from official listings. However, figures for land areas are of dubious reliability for many regions where no accurate surveys have been made. Some of the figures for areas in Melanesia have been rounded off and are obviously approximations. In other regions figures to two decimal points, nevertheless, may be just as unreliable, particularly where they refer to aggregations of numerous tiny bits of land on atoll reefs. Here, also, few ground surveys have been made, and estimates of area generally are made from old charts or from maps made from aerial photographs. The scale of these charts and maps is so small and the land itself in such small bits that the percentage of error becomes inordinately large. Moreover, it is hard to determine how much of a bare patch of rubble on a reef should be considered "land," since the high tide line is not always readily discernible when charts are made from aerial photographs. As an instance of the variances, although the official land area for the Tuamotu group is reported at 330 square miles, Dr. Kenneth Emory of the Bishop Museum, Honolulu, who is personally familiar with the area, believes the actual land surface could not be more than seventy-five square miles.[1]

In the statistics on population, an attempt has been made where possible to provide two sets of figures about a decade apart in order to provide a basis for the calculation of population growth rates in recent years. Usually the statistics of the later of the two dates is the more accurate, for in many areas the recording and gathering of statistics has only recently been systematized.

NOTEWORTHY OBSERVATIONS

Assuming all the figures to be nearly correct, many noteworthy observations may be derived from the table. One is the small total area of land involved in the American administered sectors of the Pacific, especially when the areas of the Aleutian and Hawaiian groups are excluded. A second aspect is the great disparity of population densities on the different islands and island groups of the Pacific. There are such differences as the 7-9 persons per square mile on the Solomons, New Hebrides, and New Caledonia, and the 1012 per square mile in the United States administered sections of the Ryukyu Islands.

A third aspect is the great disparity in the rates of population increase going on in the different groups and islands, from as much as 7 per cent per annum in the Marianas to as little as 0.58 per cent per annum in New Hebrides. Accompanying this aspect is the rapid increase in population densities on many islands and

[1] Freeman, O., *Geography of the Pacific*, 1951, 380.

island groups and the slowness of increase on others. In the case of the Marianas the rise is 44.5 per cent in 10 years, in the case of American administered Ryukyus 36 per cent, and at Kusaie Island over 51 per cent. On the other hand, the rise in density in the Tuamotus is only about 9.2 per cent during the same length of time.

These great discrepancies between different islands require some explanations. Differing densities may be the result of one or more contributing factors, such as the proportion of arable land, the degree of fertility or the suitability of the arable land for different types of crops or food plants, the climatic conditions, the types of economy practiced, the presence of military establishments providing employment and income to the local people, and the local health conditions.

The lack of data on the proportion of land usable or capable of being made usable for food production on most Pacific islands makes the first contributing factor hard to assess. Some volcanic islands are extremely lacking in level areas. On the other hand, coral atoll land generally is considered level, yet there are striking differences in the densities for the Caroline atolls which averaged 331 per square mile in 1956, and for the Tuamotus whose densities in the same year averaged only about 88.6 per square mile based upon Emory's conservative figure for the land area, or only 20.2 per square mile, based upon the official area estimate. The difference is partly attributable to the far greater rainfall of the Caroline atolls which have at least double the rainfall of the Tuamotus, a dry group of atolls.

On the other hand, in both instances apparent population pressure has led to migration of atoll people to higher islands with more land for settlement or better employment possibilities. Thus, the five atolls around Ponape in the eastern Carolines have sent hundreds of people to Ponape. Whereas the population of the Caroline Islands as a whole increased in ten years from 35,994 in 1948 to 48,446 in 1958, the population of the atolls in the group decreased from 9496 to 8137 during the same period. A large part if not all of this decrease probably has resulted from migration to the larger volcanic islands with vacant land for homesteading.

Similarly, in the Tuamotus the population movement has been to metropolitan Tahiti in the Society group. Within the United States Trust Territories, the Marshall atolls are much less densely populated than the Caroline atolls. Although there are aridity factors in the northern Marshalls reducing potentials for population, there appears to be a genuine difference in population pressure between these groups. On the same standard of living the Marshalls could support a far greater population than they do, whereas for many of the Caroline atolls the land is overpopulated. Thus, Kapingamarangi in 1954 supported some 430 people on its 276 acres of land surface, almost the equivalent of 1000 people per square mile of area.

POPULATION-SUPPORT CAPACITIES OF ISLANDS

Since coral atoll land comprises chiefly limestone with very little humus, it is generally assumed that their soils are less productive than the soils of volcanic islands. Yet a comparison between the densities of volcanic islands and atolls would seem to indicate the greater potential for population support of atolls per unit of land surface. However, the explanation more likely is that since these figures are based upon gross areas, and since volcanic islands have a large proportion of their surfaces in steep slopes unsuitable for growing food plants, only a small portion of most Pacific volcanic islands are arable. By contrast, most of the gross area of coral atoll land in wet climates can support coconut palms.

Moreover, in considering the carrying capacity of an island for population, the importance of the sea, lagoon, and reef area must not be overlooked. This is also important in comparing the livelihood situation of inland versus coastal inhabitants on the larger islands. Those that have access to the sea for their canoes and boats, or who own land adjoining the reef, can supplement their land-derived foods with marine foods. An atoll lagoon provides sheltered waters for fishing that make a vital difference to atoll inhabitants. For instance, the ex-Bikini atoll people were moved from their atoll with its well-stocked lagoon and extensive reefs to Kili, a reef islet without any lagoon. This change greatly reduced the amount of fish and other marine foods which they could obtain. It has caused them to have to rely to a much greater extent upon the land plants, upon the few pigs and chickens that such an island can support and upon imported foods paid for by their subsidy funds. Fortunately, the Kili land has a much greater rainfall and provides a far more luxuriant plant life and more productive coconut plantations than Bikini ever could.

In general, the capacity for population support per square mile of atoll land depends not only upon the rainfall, but also upon the extent of lagoon and the extent of live reefs. Mere comparisons of the land surfaces of atolls do not provide a good index to the density of population that an atoll can support. This also applies to coastal lands of volcanic islands with barrier reefs.

COMPARATIVE POPULATION DENSITIES

When contrasted with any of the other island groups in the Pacific, the Ryukyus appear densely populated. This density derives both from natural conditions and the culture of these islands. The subtropical moist monsoon climate provides conditions suitable for a great variety of food crops. East Asiatic methods of intensive crop culture, especially of rice and sweet potato, and the practice of organic fertilization from night soil leads to a relatively high per unit area productivity. This makes possible the high population density.

By contrast, such island groups as the Mariana and Palau archipelagoes must be considered rather underpopulated in terms of their potentials. Thus, during the period of the Japanese Mandates, Tinian and Saipan supported 28,500 Japanese and Okinawans in various occupations, mostly in farming. The Palaus supported almost 24,000 Japanese civilians during 1940 in addition to the fewer than 6000 Palau natives. In 1958, therefore, the Marianas and Palaus each supported only about one-fourth of their 1940 populations. This is important in considering what is to be done about present areas of high population pressure and the future increase of population in the United States Trust Territories.

REVERSAL OF AND RISE IN POPULATION TRENDS

Only a few decades ago there still were gloomy predictions about the rapid decline and imminent extinction of the native populations of Micronesia, Polynesia and Melanesia. This decline set in rapidly after 1800. Polynesians who were estimated once to number as many as a million have been reduced to about 200,000; Melanesians have been reduced from an estimated 3,000,000 to one-third this number, Micronesians from some 270,000 to only about 100,000. Among the reasons for this remarkable decline were the hitherto unknown infectious diseases brought into the Pacific islands by whalers, traders, explorers and missionaries. Contributing causes were the already prevalent poverty and certain social practices which increased the devastating character of some of the diseases. Also, before missionary influence changed the social attitudes, abortion and infanticide were widely practiced. Malnutrition contributed to abnormally high infant mortality.

Today, however, social attitudes have changed completely, and children are much desired and much loved. Even illigitimate children are generally assured of quick adoption, and there is no stigma attached to such children. It is probable that the introduction of European type clothing in the hot humid tropics and early missionary insistence that women be completely covered led to health hazards. This was not so much because of the clothing of the body, but because of such native practices as bathing without taking the clothes off and letting the clothes dry on the body, a good way to produce a chill. Clothes frequently were not washed at all or not washed often enough. Of course, soap always has been a luxury in the islands, and on atolls fresh water often is too scarce to be used freely for clothes-washing.

The drastic reductions that occurred in some of the island groups are indicated by the Spanish estimates of native populations of between 60,000-100,000 in the Marianas, which before the end of the century became reduced to fewer than 2000. Early European estimates of Marquesan populations reached between 100,000 and 200,000. By 1813 the estimates had dropped to 50,000, and in 1842 this had dropped further to 20,000. In 1872 there were reported to be only 6200, and in 1926 only 2283.

In the Marshall atolls the population before the German occupation was estimated at some 15,000, but at the time of the German occupation the population was estimated to be 2000-3000 less. By 1911 the estimated population was 9163. In a like manner, the population of Truk is estimated to have dropped from 35,000 in 1827 to only 9510 in 1948; that of Ponape from 15,000 in 1820 to only 1705 in 1891; and that of Yap from 40,000 in 1783 to only 2744 in 1948.

Undoubtedly, the earliest figures are the least reliable and may be considerably exaggerated. There is no doubt concerning the drastic decline of population during the 19th century, however. This decline appears to have stopped by the beginning of World War I, and in most island groups the native populations were on the rise.

In a number of islands there was a period where the native populations were stationary. In 1927 such islands as Tahiti, the Fijis, the Loyalties, Rotuma and Rapa had Polynesian populations that appeared to be just maintaining themselves. Until the period of the Japanese Mandates, the Micronesian populations of most of the Carolines appeared to be static and the decline of the Marshallese seemed to have slowed down. At the same time, the Kusaien and Marianas populations were showing a tendency to increase.

From Table I in the foregoing pages, it is clear that currently the era of increase in Pacific islands population is well underway. In fact, the rate of population increase in many areas is astonishingly and even alarmingly high. In the United States administered islands American Samoa and Yap, with 1.4 and 1.57 per cent annual increase respectively, are among the slowest-growing populations, and these are not far behind continental United States rates of growth of around 1.8 per cent. Possibly lower is that of the Caroline atolls, whose total population for the decade previous to 1958 showed a decline, but since emigration figures largely in this decline, the natural growth rate is unknown.

Lack of detailed data prevents explanations for such fantastic average annual increase rates as the 7.3 per cent for the Marianas, the 5.7 per cent for Kusaie, and the 5 per cent for the Palaus. In the case of the Marshalls, with 3.56 per cent, and the Trust Territory as a whole, with 3.89 per cent increase, no outside immigration would be involved to complicate the picture, which is one of an extremely high rate of natural increase. In terms of the limitations of island land for food production, these rates, if continued, could truly be described as explosive.

The reason for such marked rises cannot be certainly stated without intensive field investigations, but some reasons may be suggested. Improvements in sanitation and health practices achieved through education, increased medical and hospital facilities, the training of medical aides stationed on the different islands, immunization programs and, in many cases, improvement in nutrition, all probably have been contributing influences. The limiting of unrestricted entry by outsiders who unwittingly carry infectious diseases also has limited the spread of disease. No doubt, too, through the process of natural selection and survival of the fittest, those that have survived to carry on the line have acquired an increased immunity and resistance to diseases.

The change in the population trends not only shows a revitalization of the Pacific racial stocks but must arouse concern lest unchecked increase in the future results in depriving the inhabitants of effective productive resources for raising their standards of living to the rising expectations deriving from a greater awareness of Western standards. Under present United States laws, the population of the Trust Territory is not free to migrate to the United States for permanent residence. Nor are there other lands open to them for settlement where they may make a suitable livelihood.

INEQUALITIES IN ISLAND POPULATION PRESSURES

Within the Trust Territory there exist great inequalities in population pressures and population support capacities. Some areas such as Mokil, Pingelap, and Kapingamarangi are overcrowded. It might appear that a temporary remedy might be to re-settle these people where the population is sparse compared with the food-producing land. Only to a limited extent is this possible. Land on all the islands is community or privately owned except for certain limited areas of land appropriated by the administrative powers, usually land which was declared public domain by the Germans or taken for use by the Japanese and now inherited by the present administration. Some of these lands are being used for homesteading by islanders from overpopulated areas.

Although the Marshalls are sparsely populated by comparison with the atolls of the Carolines, the Marshallese would not be likely to consent to Carolingian immigration into the Marshalls for settlement in significant numbers. Even in the resettlement of fewer than 100 former Bikini inhabitants, the Trust Territory administration had difficulty providing suitable land within the Marshalls.

Within the Carolines, problems of land ownership and land-use rights are further complicated by linguistic and ethnographic differences. Fortunately, on the larger islands of Ponape, Truk and the Palaus, the administration has considerable areas that can accommodate a limited number of additional settlers. Possibly the numerous uninhabited Marianas Islands may serve this purpose also, although the lack of level land caused them to be shunned even by the Japanese during the period of the Mandates. The cultural incompatibility among different groups is illustrated by the fact that some 200 Chamoros born and raised in the Palaus during the Japanese administration found the Palauan social atmosphere so uncongenial that they were glad to have the administration move them for resettlement in the Marianas.

It is clear, therefore, that the great upsurge in population growth in the Pacific islands must concern those in charge of the future of the island peoples. Most of the problems already serious to the small populations of today, such as those of health and medical services, education, communication, transportation, and the limited sources of food and income, will become magnified with further increase in population. Solutions to these problems are not readily apparent.

XI *The United States as Trustee of the Pacific Islands*

In evaluating the role of the United States as trustee of the Pacific islands of Micronesia, it is necessary to recognize the conditions under which the United States took over control. The United States, with the full knowledge and consent of the United Nations, took over these islands as officially designated "strategic trusteeships". This was done for no other reason than for their strategic and military importance. Under these terms, the United States has the right to fortify them as the United States see fit. These are very different terms from those under which the islands were mandated to Japan by the former League of Nations, terms which Japan violated when she fortified various of the Micronesian islands.

UNITED STATES RIGHTS AS TRUSTEE

Under the Trusteeship Agreement, the United States can bar from the areas within the Trusteeship anyone it chooses, including representatives of the United Nations. This is obviously a necessary condition for a strategic trusteeship, otherwise representatives of hostile great powers including the Soviet Union could use their position to gain access for intelligence purposes. The barred areas in the Trusteeships are not subject to inspection or to use by forces of other nations. Where the nuclear bomb tests were held, at Eniwetok and Bikini for instance, unauthorized persons may not visit. These were designated closed areas. This also was done for the northern Marianas which were declared closed on January 1, 1953, when their

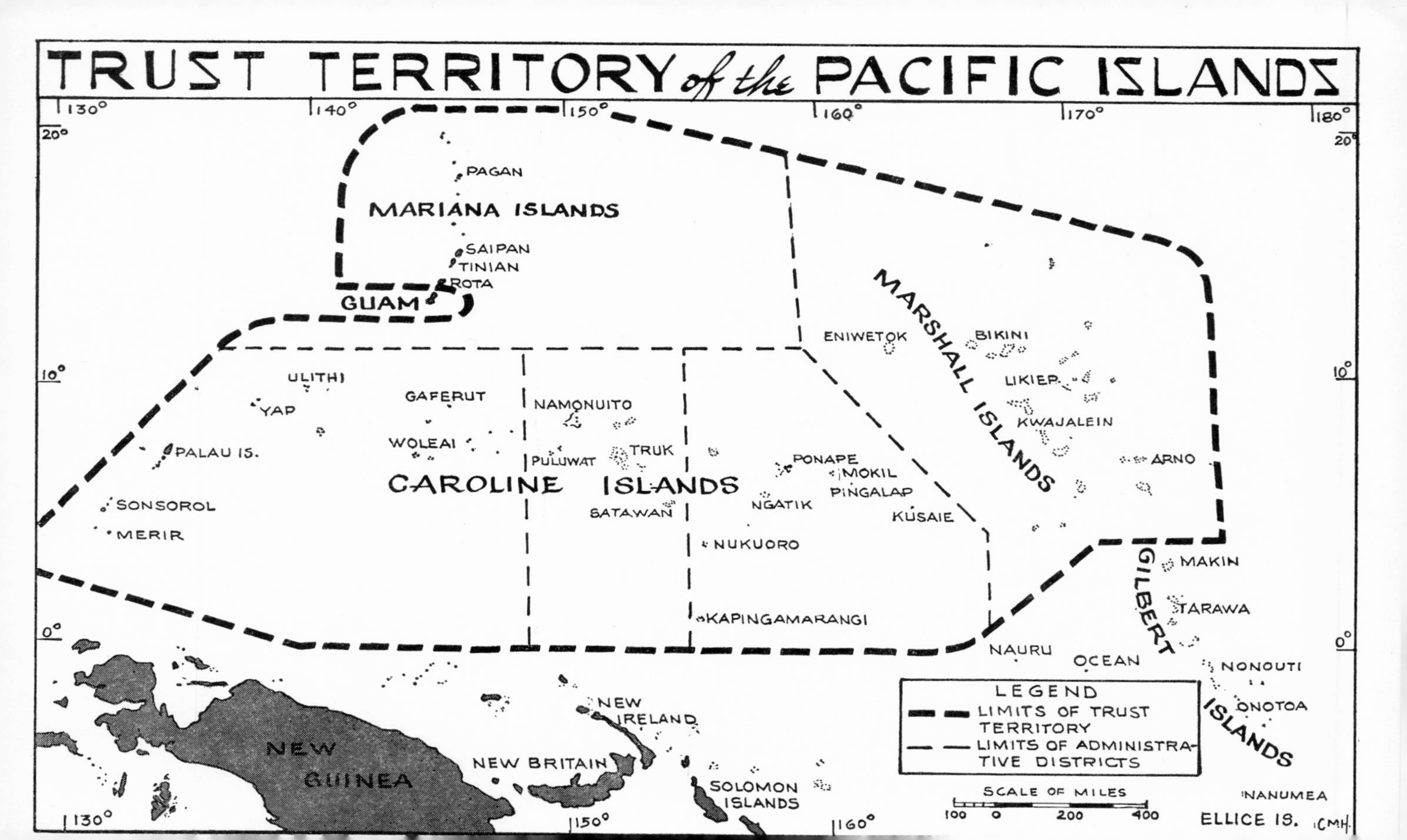
TRUST TERRITORY of the PACIFIC ISLANDS
130°
140°
150°
160°
170°
180°
20°
10°
0°
PAGAN
MARIANA ISLANDS
SAIPAN
TINIAN
ROTA
GUAM
ULITHI
YAP
PALAU IS.
SONSOROL
MERIR
GAFERUT
WOLEAI
NAMONUITO
PULUWAT
TRUK
SATAWAN
CAROLINE ISLANDS
NUKUORO
KAPINGAMARANGI
PONAPE
MOKIL
PINGALAP
NGATIK
KUSAIE
ENIWETOK
BIKINI
LIKIEP
KWAJALEIN
ARNO
MARSHALL ISLANDS
GILBERT ISLANDS
MAKIN
TARAWA
NONOUTI
ONOTOA
NAURU
OCEAN
INANUMEA
ELLICE IS.
NEW GUINEA
NEW BRITAIN
NEW IRELAND
SOLOMON ISLANDS
LEGEND
LIMITS OF TRUST TERRITORY
LIMITS OF ADMINISTRATIVE DISTRICTS
SCALE OF MILES
100
0
200
400
CMH.

administration was transferred from the Interior Department to the United States Navy.

At the same time, the United States is not interested in and has no intention of colonizing the islands or making a profit from them, as Japan did. Nevertheless, a second provision of the Trusteeship Agreement gives the United States preferential treatment in commercial and economic matters, an arrangement which is not conceded to nations administering non-strategic trust territories. Thus, the United States may exclude foreign firms from bidding on harbor, port or airfield development or other public works construction. The United States also may negotiate and conclude commercial and other treaties and agreements for the Trust Territory, such as those concerning air passage rights.

UNITED STATES OBLIGATIONS AS TRUSTEE

It is well realized by the United States Congressional Committee on Interior and Insular Affairs that the trusteeship is and will probably remain an economic liability, although the cost of the administration is regarded as an inexpensive insurance premium paid for the privilege of knowing what is going on in the islands. The costs of the Trust Territory Administration and of its educational, medical, agricultural extension and other services are largely subsidized by the United States in fulfilling its pledge under Article 6 of the Trusteeship Agreement to improve the economic, political, educational and social conditions of the Micronesians and promote their development. Many Americans are recruited under civil service regulations for two-year tours of service, subject to renewals, in the various services required by the Trust Territory.

Some observers, including the writer, feel it regrettable that, in their opinion, there is a tendency among keepers of the United States Congressional purse-strings to be niggardly in providing adequate funds for the Trust Territory Administration for the development of the native economy and for cultural progress. The funds annually provided are not sufficient to be consonant with the immense problems that administration has been called upon to solve, or to maintain the dignity of the United States in the eyes of the Micronesians. In a number of areas, the shabby buildings and temporary housing and the poor port facilities and road systems of the present administration are contrasted unfavorably by the Micronesians with those of the preceding Japanese administration. Under the Japanese Mandates, the economic status of the Micronesians often was higher, even though their educational, social and political development was much more restricted. Although the Japanese exploited the island resources for their own benefit and made profits from the territory, they did develop and maintain better roads, more frequent shipping connections and better marketing arrangements, and they stimulated more employment or, at least, production under the indigenous economy. On the other hand, because the islanders were disinclined to work under the discipline required by the Japanese, most of the development was done with imported Japanese, Korean and Okinawan laborers.

FRAMEWORK OF TRUSTEESHIP ADMINISTRATION

The government of the United States Trust Territory in the Pacific is headed by a High Commissioner appointed by the President of the United States and subject to the direction of the Secretary of the Interior. Responsibility for the administration of the Marianas, with the exception of the Rota District, however, is vested in the Commander-in-Chief, United States Pacific Fleet. Under the High Commissioner the organization as of 1958 is shown in the chart on page 107.

Within this Western framework the Micronesians locally continue certain traditional patterns of government which they have evolved over centuries and which fit in with their cultural needs. Under the American administration they have been encouraged to develop an appreciation of and retention of those aspects which have proved most useful to their requirements. Democratic processes have been inherent in many groups in the Micronesian realm, although the forms and methods of expressing the common will and the system of leadership may not resemble the democratic methods of operation of Europe or the United States. At the same time, the Micronesians are being stimulated to study, select and adopt those

HIGH COMMISSIONER
DEPUTY HIGH COMMISSIONER

Political Social Economic Staff

Public defender and Counselor (at Truk)

Legal and Public Safety

Judiciary

Administration Auditor

Construction and maintenance

Finance Department

Personnel Department

Property supply Depart.

Communications Depart. (Truk)

Education Depart. (Truk)

Public Health Department (Ponape)

Rota District

Palau District

Yap District

Truk District

Ponape District

Marshall Islands District

forms and methods in Western society that would promote their development and progress along paths of self-government more adaptable to the complex demands of the contemporary world.

PACIFIC ISLAND PAROCHIALISM

Although some sociologically-minded observers deplore the transformation of what they hold to be a preferable if simple primitive society and economy into an inevitably frustrating pseudo-modern culture, this does not seem to be the attitude of the Micronesians themselves in most cases. They inescapably have become tied to the complexities of the modern world and they want a share of the satisfactions that industralization brings. They are being assisted on all levels of government to develop greater understanding and proficiency in legislative, executive and judicial functions as well as in the improvement of their agriculture and economy. This is being done through a variety of group and council meetings as well as through personal assistance to municipal and other officials. In addition to meetings of District Administrators with local councils and congresses, a Territory-wide conference of representative Micronesian leaders chosen from local congresses and councils have met upon several occasions at the Administration Headquarters at Guam.

The objective of this educational process is to overcome the strong parochialism and feelings of insularity among the inhabitants of the various islands and to produce a Territory-wide sense of political and societal unity among the leaders. Island loyalties have a restricted range which complicates the task of building an administration staffed by Micronesians and greatly limits the rate of progress toward self-government beyond a local level. Although large segments of the island population share some sense of common regional identity in terms of language, history and culture, this does not imply political unity even on individual island groups or, as in the case of Ponape, even on a single island. An example illustrating this from so American-acculturated a group as the Marshallese is a petition submitted by a group of them to a visiting United Nations Mission in 1953, part of which stated:

> We understand and appreciate the American ideal of "one people", but we are a separate country from Ponape, with our own separate customs and culture and language and have no more desire to be classed with or merged with the Ponapeans than France has desire to merge with Germany or China with Japan. We feel that it is unfair to us as a people to be lumped together with other groups of Micronesian peoples as one people. We are proud of our race and our heritage and fear any attempt to merge us culturally or otherwise with other peoples with the resultant loss of our own culture and individuality.

What is not yet widely realized among the Micronesians is the necessity for pooled effort by all the islands if the Micronesians are to achieve a more viable economy and the goals that most of them would like to see accomplished for their various communities. On the other hand, it may be that some see as unrealistic the effort to accomplish such goals without the subsidization by the superior resources of a major power and prefer to remain subsidized wards of a trustee power.

OBSTACLES TO UNITY OF ISLAND COMMUNITIES

It is certainly true that political unification under a Territory-wide Micronesian administration not only faces obstacles of provincialism, but also the very real one of communications, both in the linguistic and in the transportation fields. There is a multitude of different languages spoken. This is not unique, of course, for many countries of Asia—for example, India—have this problem. In the case of the Trust Territory of Micronesia, there is not even one overwhelmingly dominant native tongue. A few of the Micronesians of each locality traditionally have used the language of their governing power as a lingua franca. During the German administration, the Micronesians had to learn German to communicate with their rulers. Then a succeeding generation or two had to learn enough Japanese to get along with the Mandate administration. Now the rising generations are learning English. English has become the only language for widespread intercommunications.

As knowledge of English is increasingly fostered by the intermediate levels of the school system, inter-regional understanding and cooperation should increase and parochialism decrease. This is a slow process, however. Only a limited number of Micronesian school children at present go to school beyond the vernacular levels of their home community (usually about the 6th grade level in the American school system). Moreover, it takes many years for the younger members of society to gain standing in leadership in their home communities. On the other hand, many of this new generation are being absorbed into the ranks of the Trust Territory administration and are getting trained in the techniques of American education and government. As these Micronesians assume more and more skill and practical responsibility, their enhanced prestige leads to their emergence as political leaders. Consequently, the leadership of the traditional chiefs becomes increasingly more ceremonial and decreasingly practical. These opportunities encourage the sending of young persons of special ability to more advanced levels of schooling and training at Guam, Fiji, Honolulu and the United States.

REMOTENESS OF UNITY AND INDEPENDENCE

To look farther ahead into the future, one might ask whether ultimately an independent state of Micronesia may not emerge that would gather all the islands within a democratic framework. The answer would appear to be that the practicality of this still lies in a very remote future.

The problems of independence are far greater than the problems of a Territory-wide unification, although to a large extent these problems also underlie unification itself. They are mainly those concerned with costs of communications and transportation. The small amount of surplus that can be produced above subsistence needs and the limited types of production and resources make the economy incapable of supporting the minimum needs of the population for education, medical care and a standard of living that has the expectations of even the present modest levels. Much of the cost of satisfying these needs arises from the long distances that transportation must span between small scattered communities. Most of the islands even now see a ship sail into harbor only about once in one, two, or three months.

The mere process of gathering together the Marshallese Congress, for instance, is a staggering and time-consuming problem, even when the Trust Territory Administration provides vessels to send around to collect the delegates free of charge and provides free food allowances to them during the Congress. Without such subsidization, there would be no Marshallese Congress, and it would be hard to persuade an islander of the advantages of suscribing funds to send delegates to it, not to mention to even more remote Territory-wide congresses.

CONTINUED DEPENDENCE UPON THE UNITED STATES

The responsibilities and costs of independence and self-government may be theoretically desirable, but practically, the Micronesians would much prefer a protector power to assume these costs in return for whatever advantages it sees in assuming the governing power. As far as indications have been given to American or outside observers, the Micronesians of the Trust Territories, while having some grievances, would not like to change the American regime for any other. They are content to develop their economic and political life with American help and under American guidance and protection.

There is thus a reasonable expectation that the scattered land areas of the Pacific and Micronesia east of the Asiatic Islands will continue to strengthen their bonds with the United States and that selected islands will retain their importance in the strategic network of our Pacific bastions for an extended and indefinite future. Such long-term bonds demand a greater interest than has been accorded by the United States Administration and the United States Congress in the physical plant of the Trust Territory Administration and in the economic modernization of the Pacific islands under United States jurisdiction and protection.

XII The Islands in Pacific Communications

ASIDE from the military importance of the Pacific islands, they are also of strategic value in commercial maritime and air transportation. In these roles they serve not only as refueling and re-supply stops, but also as origins and destinations of freight and passenger movements.

SEA COMMUNICATIONS

The principal Pacific shipping routes have long been established. In the Pacific east of the Asiatic island chains, Honolulu is the great cross-routes of sea lanes and air routes. Six major-tonnage sea-routes radiating from Honolulu lead to Seattle (and nearby Vancouver), San Francisco Bay, Panama Canal, Yokohama (and other Japanese ports), Sydney, Australia and Auckland, New Zealand. About a dozen lesser-tonnage routes lead to other ports around the Pacific rim.

The importance of the Hawaiian Islands as a trans-Pacific stop for shipping is indicated by the fact that in 1960, some 2,064 ships from overseas entered Hawaiian ports, mainly Honolulu, but including Hilo and Kawaihae on Hawaii Island, Kahului on Maui and Nawiliwili on Kauai Island. These vessels entered with 3,773,000 tons of cargo and cleared with 2,095,000 tons.

The great circle route between northwest North America and East Asia, running past the Aleutian Islands, is the largest commercial-tonnage sea-lane of all. Along this route it is 4,255 nautical miles from Yokohama to Seattle and 4,536 to San Francisco.

Lesser axial cross-routes of sea-lanes occur at Apia in Western Samoa, Tahiti in the Societies, Suva in the Fijis and Wellington in New Zealand. A minor one is at Guam.

The chief sea-lanes radiating from various axial islands and the distances to their termini are given in the following Table III:

Table III

Sea-lanes from Honolulu

Destination	Nautical miles	Destination	Nautical miles
Seattle	2,409	Cape Horn	6,370
San Francisco	2,091	Tahiti	2,381
Panama	4,685	Melbourne	4,942
Yokohama	3,394	Sydney	4,420
Suva	2,776	Guam	3,337
Apia	2,260	Manila	4,767
Los Angeles	2,228	Hong Kong	4,857
Callao	5,161	Petropavlovsk	2,762
Valparaiso	5,919		

Sea-lanes from Apia

Destination	Nautical miles	Destination	Nautical miles
Yokohama	4,057	Wellington	1,961
Guam	3,080	Panama	5,710
Sydney	2,355	Tahiti	1,301
Auckland	1,581	Magallanes, Chile	5,207

Sea-lanes from Tahiti

Destination	Nautical miles	Destination	Nautical miles
San Francisco	3,360	Wellington	2,348
Panama	4,486	Sydney	3,308
Auckland	2,216		

Sea-lanes from Suva

Destination	Nautical miles	Destination	Nautical miles
Auckland	1,149	Sydney	1,738

AIR COMMUNICATIONS

The construction of air bases during the Pacific War in 1943-1945 had an important influence upon commercial air service development in the Pacific islands in the post-war era. Among the former war-time Pacific air bases constructed by the United States that were in commercial use in 1960 were the following:

Table IV

South Pacific	*Central Pacific*
Bora Bora, Society Islands	Honolulu, Oahu
Tafuna, Tutuila, Samoa	Hilo, Hawaii
Apia, Western Samoa	Canton Atoll
Wallis Island	Majuro Atoll
Noumea, New Caledonia	Guam Island
Espiritu Santo, New Hebrides	Wake Atoll
Honiara, Guadalcanal	
Munda, New Georgia	
Southwest Pacific	*Alaska*
Merauke, New Guinea	Adak
Port Moresby, New Guinea	Amchitka
Samarai, New Guinea	Annette
Lae, New Guinea	Attu
Finschhafen, New Guinea	Cold Bay
Manus Island Group (Los Negros Is.)	Dutch Harbor
Hollandia, Western New Guinea	Kodiak
Biak, Schouten Eilanden	Shemya
Western New Guinea	Umiat

Those in the South and Southwest Pacific, with the exception of Tafuna, are not on United States controlled territory, and Canton Atoll is jointly administered by the United States and the United Kingdom. Nevertheless, all of these bases are in territory controlled by allies of the United States. In fact, the only air bases in the entire Pacific operated by a power hostile to the United States are Soviet bases on Kamchatka Peninsula, on Sakhalin and on the islands in the Kurile chain.

INFLUENCES ON DISTRIBUTIONAL PATTERNS

Influences affecting the distributional pattern of commercial air routes in the Pacific are the existence of airfields at certain localities, the location of population centers, the adequacy of surface transport, national considerations and aircraft range. The war-time construction have made many airfields available in many areas where the amount of commercial traffic now using them would not have justified their construction. Traffic frequency between populated places is more important than the mere existence of large population centers. This accounts for the concentration of routes across the northern and western Pacific and their absence in the southeast Pacific. The absence of rapid sea transport over wide ocean expanses is one important factor in establishing air routes between more important centers within the oceanic areas.

National considerations are expressed in the form of subsidies, mail and other government contracts to carriers. This permits airlines to operate where they could not do so profitably in a purely commercial way. Examples of this are the weekly Trust Territory round-trip air services between Guam, Yap and the Palau Islands, and between Guam, Truk, Ponape and Majuro. In the Aleutians, the routes west of Cold Bay are little used by civilians but exist chiefly to serve the military bases. Similarly, the Military Air Transport Service route from the San Francisco Bay area to Honolulu, Kwajalein, Guam and Manila serves United States Government and military needs.

Aircraft range is another important influence in the distributional pattern of Pacific air routes. This is especially important in the locations of long trans-Pacific hops with few islands to serve as refueling stops. The increase in aircraft range has reduced the dependence upon intermediate stops, however. For instance, in the case of a trans-Pacific service from San Francisco to Hong Kong, the stops it once made at Midway, Wake, Guam and Manila have been eliminated, and Tokyo has become the intermediate stop between Honolulu and Hong Kong.

Wake and Canton Atolls serve as refueling points but not ordinarily as points of traffic origin. Such islands as Honolulu and Guam serve both functions. With the development of planes that can range half-way around the world now a distinct commercial possibility, aircraft range will be eliminated as an important consideration in routing planes, just as high altitude flying has eliminated weather as a determining factor. However, the existence of certain prevailing high-altitude wind directions and jet streams will continue to influence the routing of airplanes to take advantage of their additional push or to avoid their opposition. This is illustrated by the flight routes between Honolulu and East Asiatic points. The first segment, Honolulu to Wake, has 16 westbound flights and only 11 eastbound. The reason for this difference in the number of flights in each direction is that the through flights which diverge at Wake Island to Tokyo return to Honolulu direct to take advantage of favorable winds.[2]

PACIFIC AIR TRANSPORT PATTERNS

As of January 1960 no commercial flights were made across the Pacific from any coastal points in the Americas south of Los Angeles. From Los Angeles northward, commercial trans-Pacific flights were made from six other air terminals in addition to Los Angeles. In order of significance in terms of number of flights per week, these seven take-off points were San Francisco, Los Angeles, Portland, Anchorage (Alaska), Seattle, Vancouver and Kodiak (Alaska). Five of these take-off points sent planes to Honolulu, which is the hub of Central Pacific air communications. One of these (from Kodiak Island) was minor, sending flights to Honolulu only once a month, although both Kodiak and Anchorage sent planes island-hopping westward along the Aleutian chain. Vancouver, the second-least important, sent four flights weekly. Portland, however, sent and received 14 flights weekly to and from Honolulu, or twice daily as a rule. Between Honolulu and Los Angeles 29 flights moved each way weekly, and between Honolulu and San Francisco there were 35 weekly flights westward and 33 flights eastward.

Two of the seven continental take-off points also sent flights non-stop to Tokyo, the most important trans-Pacific terminal in the West Pacific. From Anchorage 13 flights went to Tokyo which sent 14 return flights weekly. From Seattle 10 flights went to Tokyo which sent back 9 flights. Tokyo also sent two flights non-stop to San Francisco, but San Francisco did not originate non-stop com-

[2] William L. Thomas, Jr., Richard I. Gates, Pacific Air Transport, Library Brochure prepared for the Pacific Missile Range, Point Mugu, California, 30 December 1960.

mercial flights for Tokyo in 1960. This may be because of contrary high altitude winds.

From Honolulu, in addition to the flights to the continental North American west coast, there were six flight routes radiating westward and southward. The major trunk line was that reaching to Wake Island with 16 westbound flights and 11 eastbound on this route. From Wake nine of the westward flights diverged to Tokyo and seven (one a day) ran to Guam. From Guam there was a further forking of flight lines, with two flights weekly to Okinawa and five flights weekly to Manila, each of which sent back the same number of return flights, which then continued from Guam to Wake to Honolulu. Tokyo sent four flights weekly to Honolulu via Wake Island and 12 non-stop flights directly to Honolulu, which sent 9 weekly non-stop flights to Tokyo.

In a southerly direction, the chief air route is that between Honolulu and Nandi in the Fiji Islands, with six flights weekly each way. Weekly flights each way also occurred between Honolulu and the two termini of Bora Bora and Tafuna. An additional weekly flight between Honolulu and Tafuna was routed via Canton Atoll. Weekly flights also connected the Societies with the Fijis both direct and routed through Tafuna and Apia in the Samoan Islands.

Nandi is a secondary hub in the South Pacific. From here the two chief air routes connect Nandi with Auckland, New Zealand, and Sydney, Australia, each route with five flights weekly each way. Weekly flights also run between Nandi and Noumea in New Caledonia, which is connected by weekly flights with Brisbane, Sydney and Auckland, as well as with Espiritu Santo and nearby small islands. Air routes run the length of northern New Guinea, and this route connects both with Guadalcanal in the Solomons and with Australia via Port Moresby in southeastern New Guinea. Both from Port Moresby and from Biak in northwestern New Guinea, there are lines running to Manila, another major hub of air traffic in the West Pacific, with frequent connections with Japan, Taiwan, Okinawa, Hong Kong, Bangkok, Saigon and weekly flights to Djakarta.

XIII The Pacific Islands in the Nuclear and Missile Age

CHANGES in technology and weaponry must affect strategic evaluations, and it is reasonable to ask the question whether island bases are not obsolete in the nuclear and missile age.

It has been observed that the decision to retain Micronesia after the Pacific War probably rested on the shock of Pearl Harbor and on the large casualties suffered by the United States in the capture of the islands, rather than on calculation of strategic needs. It is true that the strategic value of these islands to the United States after 1945 certainly was different and possibly less significant than it would have been had the United States possessed them prior to 1941. It seems safe to say, too, that the present strategic value of these islands has changed from that of the immediate postwar period, and that there will continue to be re-evaluations of their role in the future.

BASE VULNERABILITY IN THE NUCLEAR AGE

When the United States decided to take over control of the former Japanese Mandates, the nuclear age had just blazoned over the horizon, and potential enemies of the United States did not then possess either nuclear weapons or the long range missiles for accurate delivery. Since then, the Soviet Union has demonstrated that it can send a missile from its interior launching sites and hit within several miles of its target area in the Central Pacific. It would seem to be even easier for it to launch nuclear missile attacks against any of the islands of the Pacific from its maritime Pacific coasts or from the China coast. No longer does an enemy on the west Pacific peripheral have to sail aircraft carriers secretly to within a few hundred miles of Hawaii to launch aircraft to blast Pearl Harbor. Even were long-range ICBM weapons not sufficiently precise, it would be virtually impossible to detect hostile submarines before they reached easy missile range for sending a nuclear bomb with accuracy to devastate Pearl Harbor and Honolulu. This would apply to any other island base.

CONTINUED IMPORTANCE OF ISLAND BASES

On the other hand, this no more invalidates Pacific island bases than it invalidates continental bases, since the latter have become only a little less vulnerable. From a nuclear war viewpoint, some of the same criteria justify island bases as justify fixed continental bases. The more separate bases there are, the more problems they present to an enemy intent on destroying or neutralizing them. From another viewpoint, if there is a justification for a navy or an air force, there must be bases to service and maintain them. In this respect, the Pacific islands with existing or potential facilities continue to have a strategic role. Also, as long as the concept of limited warfare is thought to be valid, the Pacific islands must be included in strategic planning. In fact, in the practical business of the "cold war" and the limited "small wars" such as those that took place in Korea, Vietnam and Laos, or in the continuing task of strengthening and reassuring our East and Southeast Asian and Southwest Pacific allies, some of our Pacific islands are logistically indispensable.

Certain of the islands possess three other potential or existing functions: (1) as sites for weather stations; (2) as launching and/or tracking stations for missiles and space satellites; (3) as bases for surveillance of the seas for movements of hostile submarines. With the existence of a large Soviet submarine fleet and the growing submarine force of Communist China, the latter function becomes more than an academic problem. The American missile-tracking radar stations in Hawaii, Kwajalein and the Aleutians have given the United States invaluable information on the development of

Soviet missiles. Kwajalein now also is the site of an important missile base.

THE NEED FOR BASE DISPERSAL

On the other hand, to regard excellent island harbors as bases where vast numbers of fleet units may be concentrated would be a perilous concept. In the event of nuclear warfare between the United States and an enemy in the Pacific, such great concentrations as were gathered at Majuro, Eniwetok or Ulithi lagoons during the Pacific War could not be assembled without great risk, for a single hydrogen bomb would wipe out or sink most of the vessels concentrated in such a small area. Dispersal into smaller units in numerous scattered harbors is the better strategy in spite of the greater logistical efforts needed and the higher base expenses involved.

This type of strategy would have to utilize many more islands in the Pacific than are now being used for base purposes. While Mahan's principle of concentration of fire-power and destruction upon a target still holds, it would appear that concentration of the means of delivery can no longer be entertained. As a military commentator has pointed out,[3] widely scattered overseas bases present the potential enemy with a problem of coordination almost impossible for him to resolve. He must attack all the bases overseas and in North America with a precision of timing that strikes all targets nearly simultaneously or lose the value of surprise that is necessary for a nuclear victory. The difficulty for the potential attacker would be compounded were it a fixed naval policy always to have a considerable proportion of its floating missile-arsenals and launching-ships on patrol at all times. This would ensure that, even were all bases simultaneously hit by nuclear bombs, the nuclear striking forces of the United States would not all be sitting ducks on the base ponds.

Such a diversity of bases, on land and afloat, makes possible a heavy and diverse attack upon the potential enemy in the event of his attempt to achieve a quick victory by surprise attack. How-

[3] Hanson W. Baldwin in the New York Times Magazine, October 9, 1960, 106.

ever, at present too many Pacific island bases have been deactivated and too much of the striking power is concentrated into too few sites.

POTENTIAL BASE READINESS

In the era of missiles and jet planes, the lightning element of the *Blitzkrieg* allows for little or no time to prepare a base for retaliatory strikes or for stopping further advances. That is, a potential base under unready circumstances is no base at all. At least the essential framework must be in existence ahead of time. Thus, for airbases, usable landing fields must be in existence currently, even if the housing, repair and service facilities related to their use be left for installation when the actual need arises. Similarly, wharfs and harbors and strategic approach highways to both airfields and ports should be readied, and water supply facilities should be currently in good condition. Many of the fine facilities, airfields, ports and roads that existed at the end of the Pacific War on the islands have been abandoned to ruin and weedy jungle. Their partial rehabilitation would ready them for quick use as logistic support bases or missile sites, or for one or more of the many other functions they might serve in case of need. At the same time, they could and should serve the transportation needs of the local populace. The stand-by maintenance of such facilities by the native islanders could provide much needed jobs and extra income for the islanders at small cost to the United States, and only occasional supervisory visits would be needed to see that maintenance was being done.

It is true, of course, that even were no military base facilities developed on most of the Pacific islands now under United States administration, their very denial to the use of potentially hostile powers is of immense strategic value to the United States, just as their danger to the United States in the hands of an enemy power was so clearly demonstrated during the Pacific War. However, although the dictates of economy have restricted the number of active bases in the Pacific islands, the needs of the missile era for virtually instantaneous activation of a widely distributed number of bases to avoid overconcentration in the event of hostilities demand partial reconstruction of many presently abandoned airstrips and port facilities on numerous Pacific islands. In view of the longer runways needed for jet aircraft, many former adequately long flight strips also would need lengthening, something which cannot be done quickly.

THE PERMANENCE OF UNITED STATES CONTROL

Another factor adding strategic importance to the Pacific islands of the United States and to the islands under their trusteeship is the permanence or relative permanence of United States control over them. In this respect, they differ from United States bases that are located by consent upon the territories of allied nations such as those in Japan, the Ryukyus and the Philippines. Although at present and for the foreseeable future the strategic security of these lands requires their close association with the United States, just as United States security needs their friendly support, it is not inconceivable that a time may come when circumstances may cause Japan and, though less likely, the Philippines to withdraw base privileges accorded the United States. Although the United States tenure on Okinawa by treaty is largely subject to the judgement of the United States, even here the United States may someday feel it preferable to withdraw if the combined feelings of the Okinawans and of the Japanese make this the prudent step to take. This necessity is not likely to arise in the Trust Territories, in American Samoa or in Guam.

ISLAND IMPORTANCE CONTINUES

The answer to the question posed at the beginning of this chapter must be that the Pacific islands continue to have vital strategic functions which the nuclear age and missile developments have changed but not decreased. In the vast reaches of the Pacific, land is scarce and often is measured in hundreds of acres rather than in thousands of square miles. Nevertheless, the value of many of the American possessions in the Pacific justifies their description as island bastions in the political and military strategy of the United States.

Bibliography

1. Beaglehole, J. C., *The Exploration of the Pacific,* London, 1934.
2. Bryan, Edwin H., Jr., *American Polynesia and the Hawaiian Chain,* Tongg Publishing Company, Honolulu, 1942.
3. Coulter, John Wesley, *The Pacific Dependencies of the United States,* The Macmillan Company, New York, 1957.
4. Cumberland, Kenneth B., *Southwest Pacific, A geography of Australia, New Zealand, and their Pacific Island Neighborhoods,* McGraw-Hill Book Company, New York, 1956.
5. Fischer, John L. and Ann M., *The Eastern Carolines,* Human Relations Area Files, New Haven, 1957.
6. Freeman, Otis W., Editor, *Geography of the Pacific,* John Wiley and Sons, New York, 1951.
7. Hobbs, William H., *The Fortress Islands of the Pacific,* J. W. Edwards, Ann Arbor, Michigan, 1945.
8. Jarrett, Lorna H., *Hawaii and Its People,* Honolulu Star-Bulletin, Ltd., Honolulu, 1933.
9. Keesing, Felix M., *The South Seas in the Modern World,* The John Day Company, New York, 1941.
10. King, Admiral Ernest J., "Our Navy at War," United States Naval Institute, Proceedings, Volume 70, 1944, 757-815.
11. Morrell, W. P., *Britain in the Pacific Islands,* Oxford at the Clarendon Press, London, 1960.

12. Potter, E.B., "The Navy's War Against Japan," United States Naval Institute, Proceedings, Volume 76, August 1950, 825-837.

13. Sharp, Andrew, *The Discovery of the Pacific Islands,* Oxford at the Clarendon Press, London, 1960.

14. Smith, Lt. Gen. Julian, "Tarawa," United States Naval Institute, Proceedings, Volume 79, 1953, 1163-1175.

15. Stevens, Russell L., *Guam, U.S.A., Birth of a Territory,* Tongg Publishing Company Ltd., Honolulu, Hawaii, 1956.

16. Trumbull, Robert, *Paradise in Trust, A Report on Americans in Micronesia, 1946-1958,* William Sloane Associates, New York, 1959.

17. United States Government, Department of State Publication 5735, *Trust Territory of the Pacific Islands, 1954,* U.S. Government Printing Office, Washington, D.C., 1955. (issued annually).

18. United States Navy, Hydrographic Office, Publication 165A, Vol. I, and Publication 166, Vol. III, 1952, *Sailing Directions for the Pacific Islands,* United States Government Printing Office, Washington, D.C., 1952.

19. Weckler, J. E., Jr., *Polynesian Explorers of the Pacific,* Smithsonian Institution War Background Studies, Number 6, January 13, 1943, Washington, D.C.

20. Wiens, Herold J., *Atoll Environment and Ecology,* Yale University Press, New Haven, 1962.

Index